END-TIMES EXPLAINED

END-TIMES
EXPLAINED

CHARLES R. THOMPSON

TISIP COMPANY

Wesley Chapel, Florida

END-TIMES EXPLAINED

Copyright © 2021 by Charles R. Thompson
Tisip Company
Wesley Chapel Fl. 33543

All scripture quotations are from the *King James Version* of the Bible unless otherwise indicated.

978-0-9833869-6-4
Library of Congress Control Number: 2021900647

Printed in the United States of America

CONTENTS

ACKNOWLEDGMENTS

I extend my deepest and heartfelt appreciation to my wife, Sandra Thompson. She has always been there, standing by my side. She was there to encourage me even when we experienced trying times. She was consistent in her prayers of wisdom, knowledge, and fortitude. Her loving attitude, enthusiasm, and spiritual assertiveness manufactured and stimulated a prolonged marriage. She sacrificed many hours of quality time. Her lack of selfishness brought about a transformation of love and mutual respect. It drew us nearer to God and closer to each other. Thanks, dear.

I would like to thank my children Melinda King, Deborah Pickett, and Sonia Azua, for enduring some of the early teachings. They donated many pain-staking hours of their time as my initial audience as I honed my skills researching and presenting this information. They listened intently, and they challenged me often. Their continual support caused me to develop a vital skillset and it stimulated a hunger and thirst for more of God's word.

I would like to acknowledge Patrick Bellaire and his lovely wife, Candyce. Together, we have spent countless hours discussing God's word. We have explored ways to present it in such a way that God gets all the glory, and individuals prosper with greater understanding. Epistle of Christ Ministries is a product of some of those discussions. Patrick suggested that I share the knowledge that I have acquired over the years with the world in a book. Thank you Patrick. Without your insistence and persistence, authorship would not have been possible.

I would also like to recognize Pastor David Jones of Ruach Ministries in Brandon, Fl. He shares his superb knowledge of the scriptures while expressing love and humility. What makes him unique is his way of exposing those little-overlooked details. Those discoveries opens up a whole new world of Biblical understanding. He expresses genuine sincerity as he teaches the underlying structure of God's Word. His teachings give new meaning to the phrase progressive revelation.

PREFACE

MOST people understand and acknowledge the truth of repentance and righteous living, but then they struggle with understanding the events leading up to the return of Christ. They want to know some of the challenges the world will undergo before transformation into the heavenly realm. They know their role as a born-again believer, but the process begins to get a little murky concerning the period preceding the Tribulation and the events following. There are many theories concerning the return of Christ. Some believe they have an understanding of the inner working and expectations associated with this event. Others don't know their role and duties before the Lord's return, nor their job description after that event.

Scripture vividly describes the events of that day as bleak and disheartening, thereby challenging the purpose of being a born-again believer. The destiny of those days overflows with tribulation, wrath, war, rumors, famine, pestilences, apostasy, etc. All of the fore-mentioned events instill a state of fear within the very being of man. Please note, anxiety isn't necessarily a bad thing. Fear should be the catalyst that initiates one faith in God's Word. One should not merely dwell on the negatives, but he should look deep within himself and realize that there is love, joy, peace, and happiness on the other side of (*through*). These trials and tribulations are just a sign that the promises in God's word are very near. It's like traveling through a tunnel of despair. Even though everything appears to be in total darkness, do not give up hope. There is a light at the end of that tunnel, and that light is Christ.

Scripture references two resurrections, a First Resurrection and a Second Resurrection. Immediately upon the completion of the First Resurrection, Jesus will return and establish His everlasting kingdom. The mortals will face challenging times, while the saints experience the fulfillment of God's promises. The earth will enjoy a Millennium period, where the mortals will not have to endure evil influences from Satan. The saints will be there to help them modify their way of thinking through this transition.

After the Millennium, there will continue to be even more challenges for the mortals. After a thousand years of peace, once again, man will find himself living in a world that's full of murder, debate, deceit, malignity, etc. Man repeatedly finds himself choosing to follow God or choosing to follow the illusions of self-righteousness. Immediately following this series of events is the arrival of the second death or second resurrection.

Many questions are initiated by man's curiosity to understand the future. This book will provide answers to all those questions It will explore and explain in detail the many events and occurrences that saturate the earth during this transitional period. It will point out the different players, locations, destinations, etc., that influence and mold individuals' hearts and minds. Many do not want to believe that there will be challenges along the way, but as any mother can confirm, after the labor pains have subsided, that's when the real joy begins.

Chapter 1

RESURRECTION THEORIES

GENERALLY speaking, there are several different viewpoints concerning God's eternal kingdom. Some aspects of His eternal kingdom are associated explicitly with the *Tribulation Period*, while others express a connection to the *Millennial Era*. Still, others are related to the Wrath of God. What these viewpoints have in common is the timing of the return of Christ. Those who avidly study End-time events, concerning the return of Christ, assumes the classification of either a Futurist or a Preterist.

Futurist

A Futurist is what the name implies. They are dispensationalist that adheres to prerequisite events that lead to the eternal kingdom. These events are both euphoric and catastrophic at the same time. There are different variations of the terms used to describe these events. Some of the names assigned to these future occurrences are Rapture, Tribulation, Second Coming, First Resurrection, Wrath, Millennium, Little Season, Great White Throne Judgment, and Eternity. Although all these terms are standard, they have a wide variety of meanings, depending upon the person's beliefs with whom you are conversing. Let's take a look at the different definitions.

- *The Rapture* is the resurrection of the saints that occurs when Christ returns. The Rapture fulfillment occurs when the saints who have previously died receive a spiritual body. All of the saints that's alive, undergoes a transformation from a physical to a spiritual body. There are differences of opinion concerning the timing of Christ's return, and some even believe in multiple Raptures.

- The *Tribulation* is a short period of unprecedented persecution on the earth that has no comparison. The timing of the Tribulation Period varies from one conversation to another. Some define it as a seven-year period that occurs just before the end of time as we know it today. Others describe it as a three and a half-year period that occurred around 70 AD.

- The *Second Coming* is the reappearance of Christ to establish His eternal kingdom. Many believe the Second Coming is a second Rapture that occurs after the Tribulation Period. Others believe the Second Coming is not a transformation of born-again believers who endured the Tribulation, but it is Christ returning with His previously Raptured saints.

- The *First Resurrection* is inclusive of the Rapture and Second Coming. It occurs when the righteous saints transform from a mortal or physical body to an immortal or spiritual body. The timing of the First Resurrection is immediately after the Tribulation Period.

- The *Wrath* is God's punishment of unrighteous individuals that took an active role in undermining the validity of Christ as Lord and Savior. Practically, everyone agrees that the Wrath is God's unprecedented punishment, but there are varying viewpoints on the actual timing of God's Wrath. Some believe that the Wrath and the Tribulation are synonymous, and others surmise it to be a brief Post-Tribulation event. Still, others believe the God's Wrath will only affect those active participants in Antichrist's regime.

- The *Millennium* is one-thousand years of unprecedented peace. It is a time when Satan is bound in the Bottomless Pit. His incarceration strips him of his authority to deceive humanity. There are differences of opinion concerning the timing of the Millennium and the length of the Millennium. The timing is controversial because some believe it has already begun, and others think it is still futuristic. The

Millennium's duration is questionable because some will argue that it is not a literal thousand years, but it's metaphorical.

- The *Little Season* is a period that occurs immediately after the Millennium. At that time, Satan would have completed his thousand-year sentence and released from the Bottomless Pit. When he is released, The Lord restores all of his previous powers and abilities, and he's free to take up residency on earth. He has not altered his plan, one iota. Once again, he seeks to deceive the nations.

- The *Great White Throne Judgment* is sometimes known as the Second Death. It is when God will administer His final judgment on all unrighteous entities and establish eternity for all the righteous individuals. It is the final judgment before the implementation of eternity.

- The *Lake of Fire* is the eternal destination of all unrighteous entities. Burning eternally in the Lake of Fire is their punishment for openly rejecting Almighty God. Not only does their punishment consists of separation and confinement, but they will also experience extreme affliction and discomfort.

- *Eternity* is a state of being. It is the promise that God made to all who believe in His Son, Jesus Christ. Eternity is experiencing perpetual life in the presence of Almighty God. It is a utopian reality that's free from all forms of unrighteousness.

Preterist

The word *Preterist* originates from *preterite*, which means a past action or experience. A Preterist is a person that believes in the completion of all End-time prophecies in the book of Revelation and the fulfillment of Daniel's seventy weeks around the year 34

AD. It is a belief system that Christ's return came into fruition around 70 AD when a Roman general named Titus destroyed the Jewish temple in Jerusalem. They adhere to the notion that the human race is living in the Kingdom of Heaven at this very moment. To them, the Millennium isn't a literal thousand-year period. It is a continuous-time that began around 70 AD. Even though some perceive the Preterist's viewpoint to be a viable theory, it also has opposing views because it further divides into Partial Preterist and Full Preterist. The Partial Preterist believes in fulfillment of only some of the End-time events, while the Full Preterists believe The Lord concluded all of the End-time events around 70 AD.

There are many scriptures used to substantiate the Preterist's viewpoints. The following are some of the scriptures that show the basis of this doctrine.

Mar. 13:1   And as he went out of the temple, one of his disciples saith unto him, Master, see what manner of stones and what buildings are here!

Mar. 13:2   And Jesus answering said unto him, Seest thou these great buildings? there shall not be left one stone upon another, that shall not be thrown down.

Mar. 13:3   And as he sat upon the mount of Olives over against the temple, Peter and James and John and Andrew asked him privately,

Mar. 13:4   Tell us, when shall these things be? and what shall be the sign when all these things shall be fulfilled?

Mat. 4:17   From that time Jesus began to preach, and to say, Repent: for the kingdom of heaven is at hand.

Mar. 9:1   And he said unto them, Verily I say unto you, That there be some of them that stand here, which shall not taste of death, till they have seen the kingdom of God come with power.

Mark 13:1-4 states that the invading soldiers will not leave one stone of the temple standing, and it is a known fact that the temple's destruction took place in 70 AD. Mat. 4:17 is a call for man to repent quickly because the kingdom of Heaven is near. Since it is now about 2000 years after the crucifixion, and Jesus stated that He would return immediately, many concluded that Jesus' return was in 70 AD, coupled with the temple's demolition. Jesus also stated in Mark 9:1 that some of the individuals that were alive during His ministry would not die until they witnessed the kingdom of God. Since man's lifespan is plus or minus 100 years, many concluded that Jesus returned during the destruction of the temple in 70 AD. They believe His return was approximately 40 years after the crucifixion, and many of those same individuals would have still been alive at that time. These are just a few of the scriptures used to support the Preterist's viewpoint.

The Bible is God's word, and it's accurate because God cannot lie (Tit. 1:2). Since God's word is always authentic, please consider this principle whenever studying the Bible. If you discover just one scripture that contradicts a doctrine or theory, then that theory or doctrine is amiss, and revision is necessary. Revelation 1:7 predicts that when Jesus returns, He will return in the clouds, and every eye will witness that event. Please note, there is no record of any kind, indicating that humanity as a whole has seen Jesus returning to earth in the clouds. One more thing to consider, John penned the book of Revelation around 95 AD; therefore, it is impossible for these events to have occurred in 70 AD. Based on the Preterist's doctrine, Revelation is a fictional writing rather than a book of prophecy.

When conversing about End-time events, several viewpoints are associated with the actual timing of Christ's return. These varying viewpoints have evolved into different doctrinal beliefs, and their respective names reflect the essential timing of Christ's return. The most common doctrines concerning the return of Jesus are Partial Preterists, Full Preterists, A-Millennialists, Pre-Millennialists, Post-Millennialists, Pre-Tribulationists, Mid-Tribulationists, Post-Tribulationists, and Pre-Wrath.

The Full Preterist is the only group categorized as a Preterist because they believe the Lord has completed all End-time Prophecy. All other groups assume that at least one future event must occur before Christ returns; therefore, their classification is a Futurist. This book will address a general description of each of these different doctrines. Note, there will be subtle differences, dependent upon the person's opinions with whom you are conversing at the time. Even though there may be slight variations, this information will better equip you with a mechanical knowledge of the different viewpoints.

Partial Preterists

Partial Preterists believe that *the Rapture* and *Second Coming* are two separate events. They believe *the Rapture* took place around 70 AD, and the *Second Coming* occurs at the end of the Spiritual Millennium. To them, the Millennium is not a literal 1000-year period; it is a dispensation of time, which ends just before eternity. In short, Partial Preterists believes that all End-time Prophecies are historical events except the return of Christ at the Great White Throne Judgment.

Partial Preterists believe the Lord bound Satan during the crucifixion of Christ. They believe the Tribulation Period began around 67 AD, and its completion was in 70 AD. They think a secret Rapture took place in 70 AD, which was the beginning of the Millennium. They do not believe the Millennium is a literal one thousand years, but they think it is the amount of time between 70 AD and the Great White Throne Judgment. They don't specifically reference a dispensation of time known as the Little Season, but they acknowledge Satan's release from the Bottomless Pit. They believe the Battle of Armageddon will take place just before the Great White Throne Judgment.

Full Preterists

The Full Preterist believes that *the Rapture* and *Second Coming* are the same events, and it took place around 70 AD. They think that all End-time Prophecies came to fruition around 70 AD, and humanity resides in the eternal kingdom or eternity at this very moment. Like the Preterists, they believe the Lord bound Satan during the crucifixion and the Tribulation Period began three and one-half years before 70 AD. They think 70 AD was a great year because it was a culmination of events. There was a secret Rapture, Satan's release from the Bottomless Pit, the Battle of Armageddon, and Eternity was underway.

Pre-Wrath

The Pre-Wrath Theory is similar to other Tribulation beliefs in that Christ's reappearance for His saints will be a two-part event. This theory maintains that there will be one event called the Rapture and another event called the Second Coming. The Rapture will take place within the last half of the seven-year Tribulation Period. Immediately after the Rapture, God will unleash His fury upon the earth. After the Wrath of God upon the world, an event called the Second Coming occurs. The Second Coming is when Jesus will return to earth with the Raptured saints to begin the Millennial kingdom. The Pre-Wrath Theory is born because many accept the idea that the Rapture materializes amid the Seven-year Tribulation but before the commencement of God's Wrath. This belief aligns itself with scripture because the saints are not to experience the wrath of God. 1 Thessalonians 5:9 states, "God hath not appointed us to wrath, but to obtain salvation."

On the other hand, the Pre-Wrath Theory isn't in total alignment with other scriptures. Rev. 11:15-18 states, "And the seventh angel sounded; and there were great voices in heaven, saying, The kingdoms of this world are become *the kingdoms* of our Lord, and of his Christ; and he shall reign for ever and ever...And the nations were angry, and thy wrath is come, and the time of the dead, that they should be judged, and that thou shouldest give reward unto thy servants the prophets, and to the saints, and them that fear thy name, small and great; and shouldest destroy them which destroy the earth." The preceding verses indicate that the timing of God's wrath is a post-resurrection of the saints. Pre-Wrath is similar to the Mid-Tribulation and Post-Tribulation theories, but there is a slight variance in the timing.

A-Millennial

The A-Millennial Theory is just as the name applies; there is no designated thousand-year reign of Christ here on earth. The Millennium is not a physical kingdom but a time of Christ's symbolic or spiritual authority. This belief suggest that Jesus is already reigning from heaven, and He began to reign in His spiritual kingdom around the year 70 AD. Humanity is living in that kingdom at this present moment. There will be an everlasting physical kingdom where Christ will reign, but it will not begin until Christ's symbolic kingdom has come to a complete end. A-Millennialists believe Christ's eternal reign begins with His reappearance, and that event is known as the *Second Coming*. They believe the Second Coming and the Great White Throne Judgment are synonymous. It suggests that Christ's symbolic kingdom will end at the Great White Throne Judgment, but His physical kingdom will never end. The following are a few scriptures supporting the A-Millennial viewpoint.

Mat. 4:17   From that time Jesus began to preach, and to say, Repent: for the kingdom of heaven is at hand.

Mat. 16:28   Verily I say unto you, There be some standing here, which shall not taste of death, till they see the Son of man coming in his kingdom.

Mat. 24:2   And Jesus said unto them, See ye not all these things? verily I say unto you, There shall not be left here one stone upon another, that shall not be thrown down.

In Matthew 4:17, Christ ordered humanity to repent because His kingdom was very near. Christ stated in Matthew 16:28 that some individuals would not die until they see Him coming in His kingdom. In Matthew 24:2, Christ warned the disciples that there would not be one stone of the temple left upon another. The A-Millennial Theory states that all of the preceding events occurred in 70 AD with the temple's destruction.

Rev. 20:4   And I saw thrones, and they sat upon them, and judgment was given unto them: and *I saw* the souls of them that were beheaded for the witness of Jesus, and for the word of God, and which had not worshipped the beast, neither his image, neither had received *his* mark upon their foreheads, or in their hands; and they lived and reigned with Christ a thousand years.

Rev. 20:5   But the rest of the dead lived not again until the thousand years were finished. This *is* the first resurrection.

Revelation 20:4-5 seems to contradict the A-Millennial viewpoint. It states that the saints will rule and reign with Christ for one thousand years. There are two points to be made. The first point is, who are the saints that are reigning with Him? The second point is that it has already been approximately 2000 years since Jesus purportedly began His reign; therefore, the A-Millennial viewpoint is not in total alignment with scripture.

Pre-Millennial

The Pre-Millennial viewpoint alleges that the resurrection of the saints is before the Millennium reign. The hypothesis is that there will be a Millennium or a literal thousand-year reign of Christ here on earth. The Millennium will begin after the resurrection of the saints in an event known as the Second Coming. The Pre-Millennial viewpoint is born because it affirms that the regeneration of the saints precedes the Millennium, as the name suggests.

Post Millennial

The Post-Millennial viewpoint alleges that the resurrection of the saints will not come to fruition until the Great White Throne Judgment. This position means that the Rapture, Second Coming, and First Resurrection are all the same event. The Post-Millennial viewpoint also suggests that the seven-year Tribulation Period and the thousand-year Millennium is non-existent. Many accept the notion that the timing of Christ's return for His saints is at the Great White Throne Judgment. At His reappearance, the saints are clothed with glorified bodies, and they will live happily ever after in His eternal kingdom.

Pre-Tribulation

The Pre-Tribulation viewpoint is that the resurrection of the saints will be in two different stages. The first phase will occur before the beginning of the seven-year Tribulation Period. This transformation is known as the Rapture, and this event can happen at any time without warning. This viewpoint provides an escape for the saints, prohibiting them from experiencing any part of the Tribulation. At the time of the Rapture, the saints will be gathered together in the air or clouds to meet Jesus. Then, they will journey to heaven for seven years, which coincides with the Great Tribulation Period. The second stage of the Pre-Tribulation viewpoint is that after the seven-year Tribulation Period, Jesus will return to earth with the saints at another event called the *Second Coming*. Jesus' return will usher in a period referenced as the thousand-year Millennium.

Mid-Tribulation

The Mid-Tribulation viewpoint is similar to the Pre-Tribulation point of view in that the resurrection of the saints will be in two different stages. There is only one difference between Pre-Tribulation and Mid-Tribulation views, which is the Rapture's timing. According to the Mid-Tribulation views, the Rapture will not occur before the beginning of the seven-year Tribulation. Instead, it will take place in the middle of the seven-year Tribulation. Because the Rapture occurs at the halfway point of the Tribulation Period, the term Mid-Tribulation was born as the identifying name of this viewpoint.

The explanation of why the Rapture will occur in the middle of the Tribulation is because Paul stated that the saint's physical bodies would change when the last trump sounds (1Co. 15:52).

There are only seven trumpets in the book of Revelation, and the seventh trumpet sounded at the midway point in the book. Because of the relative timing of the sounding of the last trumpet, the Mid-Tribulation Theory was born.

Mid-Tribulation believers assert that Christ will return for the saints and meet them in the air approximately three and one-half years after the Tribulation Period begins. The saints will have a part in the first half of the Tribulation Period but not in the second half. The second half is the most severe portion, called the Great Tribulation. The saints will travel to heaven with Christ until the completion of the last three and one-half years of the Tribulation. Then Jesus and the saints will return to earth for the next event, commonly known as the Second Coming, which is the beginning of the thousand-year Millennium.

Post-Tribulation

The Post-Tribulation viewpoint alleges that the Rapture and the Second Coming are the same events. The belief is that Christ will return for the saints after the seven-year Tribulation Period, meaning the saints will have to endure the Tribulation Period until the end (Mat. 24:13). When the trumpet sounds, Christ begins His descent to earth. The saints receive their glorified bodies and ascends to meet the Lord in the air. After all the saints congregate together with Jesus in the clouds, they will immediately return to earth, to begin reigning in the Millennium kingdom.

CHAPTER 2

JESUS' ACCOUNT

THE Apostles Paul and John come to mind whenever there is a conversation about the reappearance of Christ. These two individuals are the benchmark concerning End-time prophecies. Many scholars quote from Paul's writing in 1 Thessalonians 4:13-18 and 1 Corinthians 15:51-52. They quote John from the book of Revelation. Most people either forget or ignore what Jesus had to say about the End-times in Matthew 24. Even though this is a sensitive subject, let's examine Paul, John, and Jesus' writings.

Paul's Writings

1Th. 4:13   But I would not have you to be ignorant, brethren, concerning them which are asleep, that ye sorrow not, even as others which have no hope.

1Th. 4:14   For if we believe that Jesus died and rose again, even so them also which sleep in Jesus will God bring with him.

1Th. 4:15   For this we say unto you by the word of the Lord, that we which are alive *and* remain unto the coming of the Lord shall not prevent them which are asleep.

1Th. 4:16   For the Lord himself shall descend from heaven with a shout, with the voice of the archangel, and with the trump of God: and the dead in Christ shall rise first:

1Th. 4:17   Then we which are alive *and* remain shall be caught up together with them in the clouds, to meet the Lord in the air: and so shall we ever be with the Lord.

1Th. 4:18   Wherefore comfort one another with these words.

1 Thessalonians 4:13-18 is the scriptures used to show how Christ will return for His saints. These scriptures are the accepted view of the Rapture Theory. Oddly enough, the word *Rapture* does not appear in the KJV of the Bible, but scripture reveals the phrase *shall be caught up*, is synonymous with the word *Rapture*. 1 Thessalonians 4:17 states, "We which are alive and remain *shall be caught up* together with them in the clouds, to meet the Lord in the air." Another phrase associated with *the Rapture* is the phrase *gathered together*. Matthew 24:31 states, "He shall send his angels with a great sound of a trumpet, and they shall gather together his elect from the four winds, from one end of heaven to the other." Therefore, when you hear the word *rapture,* it is referencing the saints gathering with Christ.

These scriptures substantiate that Christ will return before the Tribulation Period, which is accepted to be the last seven years before the Millennium starts. Concerning the Tribulation Period, there are three different viewpoints associated with the return of Christ. The three perspectives are Pre-Tribulation Rapture, Mid-Tribulation Rapture, and Post-Tribulation Rapture. After close examination of 1 Thessalonians 4:13-18, nothing indicates *the timing* as to when the Rapture will take place. The only conclusion from these scriptures is that Christ will return for the saints, and they will gather with Him in the clouds. There is no way anyone can glean from these scriptures that Christ will return before, during, or after the Tribulation Period. There is no confirmation whatsoever.

> 1Co. 15:51 Behold, I shew you a mystery; We shall not all sleep, but we shall all be changed,
>
> 1Co. 15:52 In a moment, in the twinkling of an eye, at the last trump: for the trumpet shall sound, and the dead shall be raised incorruptible, and we shall be changed.

1 Corinthians 15:51-52 is the second set of scriptures used to corroborate that Christ will return for His saints. They verify that Christ will return and describes the saint's transformation from a mortal body to an immortal body. There is no reference of any

kind linking the return of Christ to the Tribulation Period. The only timer in these scriptures associated with the return of Christ is that it will happen at the sounding of the last trump (trumpet).

The idea of linking a trumpet to Christ's return opens up yet another can of worms. What is the relationship between the Tribulation Period and the trumpets? Perhaps this particular musical instrument is tied to one or several of the feasts that the Children of Israel were required to perform throughout their generations? 1 Thessalonians 4:16 mentions the trumpet, but what is its connection to Christ's reappearance? The trumpet is a component in at least one of the Jewish feasts (Feast of Trumpets. Is it also connected to the book of Revelation? After all, the book of Revelation is associated with the End-times, and it references the sounding of trumpets, seven to be exact. We can make a connection between His return and the trumpets, but we cannot definitively make a connection between His return and the Tribulation Period. The question becomes, what is the *timing* between the trumpets, the Tribulation Period, and Christ's return for His saints?

John's Writings

> Rev. 3:10   Because thou hast kept the word of my patience, I also will keep thee from the hour of temptation, which shall come upon all the world, to try them that dwell upon the earth.

Revelation 3:10 is another scripture used to support the Pre-Tribulation Theory. Often the phrase *I also will keep thee from the hour of temptation* is referenced to indicate that the saints will escape the Tribulation Period. Jesus stated that He would keep them from the hour of *temptation*, but He did not say He would keep them from *tribulation*. The words *temptation* and *tribulation* are entirely two different words, with two different meanings. Tribulation means *a state of extreme suffering,* and temptation implies *a desire to do something wrong.* The phrase *I also will keep thee from the hour of temptation* has absolutely no association with the Tribulation Period.

Rev. 4:1   After this I looked, and, behold, a door *was* opened
            in heaven: and the first voice which I heard *was* as
            it were of a trumpet talking with me; which said,
            Come up hither, and I will shew thee things which
            must be hereafter.

Revelation 4:1 is often alluded to be the Pre-Tribulation
Rapture, where Christ is calling the saints to meet Him in the air
(1Th. 4:16-17). Their basis for this assumption is that *the church* is
not mentioned anymore in Revelation after the third chapter.
Note, they are insinuating that *the church* and *the saints* are
synonymous. This obscure statement is assumed to be the Pre-
Tribulation Rapture, taking place before the breaking any seals,
sounding any trumpets, and outpouring any vials. All of this is
presumed because chapter 4 opens with the phrase *come up hither.*
This conclusion couldn't be further from the truth. This text is not
referencing the Rapture of the church.

The voice that John heard was a voice speaking directly to *him
and him only.* The voice that John heard was an invitation for *him* to
witness and record events of the future, namely the book of
Revelation. John was entering into a supernatural experience that's
identical to the one Paul encountered earlier. 2 Corinthians 12:4
states, "Paul was caught up into paradise, and heard unspeakable
words." Paul's experience in 2 Corinthians 12:4 had nothing to do
with the Rapture of the saints. Neither does John's experience in
Revelation 4:1 have anything to do with the Rapture of the saints.
This invitation was not for the saints, but it was a personal call for
John only. Remember, John was not Raptured, in the sense of
having his body changed. He merely had an out-of-body
experience, and that's when he received the information to write
the book of Revelation. Once he received this revelation, he re-
entered reality and recorded the book of Revelation. This verse is
not referencing the Rapture of the saints.

Jesus' Writings

Mat. 24:1   And Jesus went out, and departed from the
            temple: and his disciples came to *him* for to shew
            him the buildings of the temple.

Mat. 24:2   And Jesus said unto them, See ye not all these things? verily I say unto you, There shall not be left here one stone upon another, that shall not be thrown down.

Mat. 24:3   And as he sat upon the mount of Olives, the disciples came unto him privately, saying, Tell us, when shall these things be? and what *shall be* the sign of thy coming, and of the end of the world?

When Jesus addressed the End-times, it was a few days before His crucifixion. He was exiting the temple, and He mentioned to His disciples that not one stone of the temple would remain upon another. His disciples being curious responded by asking Him three questions.

1. When shall these things be?
2. What shall be the sign of thy coming?
3. What shall be the sign of the end of the world?

Jesus' statement about the scattering of stones prompted the disciples to ask Him those three questions. In the disciple's mind, they realized that Jesus was referencing the end of the world, so they asked Jesus these questions, and all of them are relating to the End-times.

Warnings about Deception

Mat. 24:4   And Jesus answered and said unto them, Take heed that no man deceive you.

Mat. 24:5   For many shall come in my name, saying, I am Christ; and shall deceive many.

There are many different viewpoints concerning the timing of Christ's return. All of them cannot be correct; therefore, some of them have to be wrong. Perhaps Jesus foreknew that there would be some discrepancies concerning His return, so He addressed that issue more than two thousand years ago. Jesus told the disciples that whatever they do, be sure to avoid deception. To ensure freedom from deceit, every individual should study the scriptures for himself. He or she should not rely upon the doctrines or opinions of any individual or organization. 2 Timothy 2:15 states, "Study to shew thyself approved unto God, a workman that needeth not to be ashamed, rightly dividing the word of truth." Studying the scriptures and rightly discerning the word of the Lord guarantees that one will not be embarrassed when Christ returns for His saints.

What Shall These Things Be?

Mat. 24:3   And as he sat upon the mount of Olives, the disciples came unto him privately, saying, Tell us, when shall these things be? and what *shall be* the sign of thy coming, and of the end of the world?

Mat. 24:6   And ye shall hear of wars and rumours of wars: see that ye be not troubled: for all *these things* must come to pass, but the end is not yet.

Jesus continued by answering their first question. He informed them that there would be wars and rumors of wars. He also insisted that they should not be troubled because conflicts and rumors of wars were not the world's end. They are only the beginning, but the end of the world would not come until sometime later. Perhaps many people thought the end of the world was upon them during World War I and World War II. The Gulf War of 1991 with Saddam Hussein also piqued the interest of multitudes of people. Because the war was originating in the Middle-east, many thought that was the beginning of the world's end.

During this book's writing, there's a lot of turmoil and unrest in the Middle East. The nations of Egypt, Libya, Tunisia, Syria, and Yemen have already experienced many uprisings, and the world is expecting many more disturbances. Perhaps this present unrest in the Middle East is the wars and rumors of wars that Jesus mentioned. At least, the theatre where these events are happening is in the right setting. All of the above nations are fighting within their borders. They are not fighting against each other.

> Mat. 24:7   For nation shall rise against nation, and kingdom against kingdom: and there shall be famines, and pestilences, and earthquakes, in divers places.

In the second decade of the twenty-first century, tensions were high between Iran, Israel, and the United States concerning Iran acquiring a nuclear weapon. There have been rumors of violence from every side. There is credible confirmation that Iran has threatened to stop the flow of oil through the Persian Gulf, and Israel backed plans to bomb the Iranian nuclear facilities. The fact that Iran is endorsed or supported by several countries leads many to believe that this sympathetic relationship is the prerequisite to forming an alliance or kingdom. Likewise, Israel is assisted by the United States to form another alliance or confederacy. Because these two unions oppose each other, it is a classic example of what Jesus meant when He spoke of *kingdoms against kingdoms.*

Usually, when someone thinks of a *nation,* the first thing that comes to mind is a sovereign country. The Strong's number for the word *nations* is #G1484. It means a race (as of the same habit), a tribe, or a people. As used in this text, the word nation is a group of people with the same ideology. Some examples that reflect the use of the word *nations,* are denominations, democrats, republicans, lodges, unions, sororities, etc. So when scripture states that nations will rise against nations, it can be referencing like-minded or opposing groups confronting each other. It's not necessarily two countries at war. The reference to the word *nations* in the above text is alluding to different religious or faith-based groups, such as Judaism, Christianity, Islam, Catholicism, etc. The phrase, *nation against nation,* would be any combination of the above religious groups or ethnic backgrounds standing in opposition against another.

Mat. 24:7   For nation shall rise against nation, and kingdom
             against kingdom: and there shall be famines, and
             pestilences, and earthquakes, in divers places.
Mat. 24:8   All these *are* the beginning of sorrows.

Jesus continues by telling the disciples that there will be
famines, pestilences, and earthquakes throughout the world during
the End-times. Take a look around, observe, and take inventory of
the social unrest in the world today. There's an escalation in food
shortages resulting in more and more little children worldwide
more frequently going to bed hungry. We're experiencing the
bombardment of many different diseases, such as cancer, aids,
chicken flu, Ebola, Covid-19, etc. Earthquakes seem to be at an all-
time high causing tsunamis and nuclear disasters. The irony of
these disasters is that they are not the end of the world, but they
are only precursors to the End-times.

Mat. 24:9   Then shall they deliver you up to be afflicted, and
             shall kill you: and ye shall be hated of all nations
             for my name's sake.
Mat. 24:10   And then shall many be offended, and shall
             betray one another, and shall hate one another.

Just when the Hebrew people think things could not get
any worse, they experience betrayal. This double-cross is more
than just a political betrayal because it encompasses their religious
views. Other religious groups who oppose the Hebrews' existence
will persecute them because of their contrasting religious beliefs.
Religious persecution will be so persuasive that it will cause many
Hebrew people to succumb to abandoning their God, causing
them to turn against their brethren.

Mat. 24:11   And many false prophets shall rise, and shall
             deceive many.
Mat. 24:12   And because iniquity shall abound, the love of
             many shall wax cold.
Mat. 24:13   But he that shall endure unto the end, the same
             shall be saved.

The world has become saturated with all types of false doctrines. Today, many preachers filter their messages so much that they only contain a hint of God's original message. They are more focused on the number of seats filled than teaching about the acts of the gospel of Jesus Christ, which led to so many individuals becoming born-again.

Another harsh reality today is the number of individuals standing in pulpits, with the number *666* tattooed on their bodies. Not only are they proudly displaying their engraved designs, but some of them are also claiming to be Jesus Christ Himself. It does not matter that these individuals are in direct opposition to Christ's teachings, because they do not suffer a shortage of followers.

> Mat. 24:13 But he that shall endure unto the end, the same shall be saved.
>
> Mat. 24:14 And this gospel of the kingdom shall be preached in all the world for a witness unto all nations; and then shall the end come.

Jesus also stated that God rewards those who remain faithful until the end. The phrase *he that shall endure until the end,* must be qualified. He's referencing all the things He mentioned previously: wars, rumors of wars, famines, pestilences, earthquakes, tsunamis, etc. Jesus made it quite clear that all of these things would be the beginnings of despair, but the end of the world is not yet. Because this is only the beginning, it implies that there is more to come.

Jesus also stated that the gospel would be preached to the entire world as a witness, so that man will know that the gospel is a reality. The end of the world will not occur until the whole world has exposure to the gospel of Christ.

Oddly enough, Jesus never mentioned anything about gathering together the saints to escape the horrible times that will come upon the earth. He promised that those that endure until the end would receive eternal life. He did not say He would gather the saints from earth to spare them from Tribulation. The gathering together will take place at the end of the Tribulation Period. It occurs after all of these catastrophes have been completed on earth. All the disasters mentioned in Matthew 24:4-14 will precede the return of Christ.

The first question the disciples asked Jesus was: what shall these things be? The first question is famines, pestilences, wars, rumors of wars, nations against nations, kingdoms against kingdoms, earthquakes, deception, and antichrists.

What Shall Be the Sign of Thy Coming?

Remember, the disciples asked Jesus when these things would happen. Jesus had already explained to them that the earth would experience global disasters, but He continued to inform them that there would be more turmoil before the end of the world.

Mat. 24:15   When ye therefore shall see the abomination of desolation, spoken of by Daniel the prophet, stand in the holy place, (whoso readeth, let him understand:)

Mat. 24:16   Then let them which be in Judaea flee into the mountains:

Mat. 24:17   Let him which is on the housetop not come down to take any thing out of his house:

Mat. 24:18   Neither let him which is in the field return back to take his clothes.

Mat. 24:19   And woe unto them that are with child, and to them that give suck in those days!

Mat. 24:20   But pray ye that your flight be not in the winter, neither on the sabbath day:

Mat. 24:21   For then shall be great tribulation, such as was not since the beginning of the world to this time, no, nor ever shall be.

Jesus explains to the disciples that the people of Jerusalem should flee from the city when they see the *Abomination of Desolation* that Daniel mentioned. He explains to them in Matthew 24:21 why they should escape from the greater Jerusalem area. Jesus warned the disciples, that when they see the Abomination of Desolation standing in the temple, they are to flee because that would be the beginning of *Great Tribulation*. All of the events recorded in Matthew 24:4-14 are just the beginning of affliction. Now things are going to be escalated exponentially because the Great Tribulation is about to begin. Please note, God warned the people to vacate Jerusalem, using their natural strengths and abilities. God isn't going to Rapture them from the earth.

It's paramount that the people flee from Jerusalem's surrounding areas as soon as they see the Abomination of Desolation. They were instructed to leave immediately and do not take anything with them. They are to depart at once, only taking the clothes on their back. He also encouraged the people to hope and pray that this event does not occur in the winter season or on the Sabbath Day. They don't want it to be in winter because they will have to leave hurriedly without proper winter attire. The reason for not desiring this event to take place on the Sabbath Day is because there is no public transportation in the greater Jerusalem area.

We now know that the Great Tribulation begins, when the people witness the Abomination of Desolation standing at the Holy Place. The question becomes, what is the Abomination of Desolation? To understand that phenomenon, we must go to the book of Daniel.

> Dan. 9:27 And he shall confirm the covenant with many for one week: and in the midst of the week he shall cause the sacrifice and the oblation to cease, and for the overspreading of abominations he shall make *it* desolate, even until the consummation, and that determined shall be poured upon the desolate.

In the book of Daniel, we see that that Antichrist will make a covenant with Israel. The duration of this covenant is for one week. In Hebrew, the word *week* means *seven*. Antichrist will make a seven-year covenant with Israel guaranteeing them safety and freedom to worship. After three and one-half years, he will break that agreement. When he breaks the covenant, Israel will no longer be allowed to have religious freedom. Antichrist will have an ingenious idea, to establish his religion and set himself above Almighty God. This new religion will be an abomination to the Jewish faith.

The word *abomination* means detestable or idolatry. The word *desolation* means to strip away by force. The phrase *Abomination of Desolation* means something stripped away by force and replaced with something that's exceedingly detestable. In short, the Jewish people will no longer be allowed to worship their God, but Antichrist compels them to worship him as their god. Being forced to worship another god is an abomination to the Jewish people, and it will lead to total desolation, both physically and spiritually.

In Matthew 24:15-21, Jesus was warning the people about the Abomination of Desolation because it is when the Jewish people are not allowed to worship the Creator of the universe and compelled to worship another god. When this event unfolds, they are to flee into the mountains because that would be the beginning of the Great Tribulation. Please note, the end of the world is still at an appointed time, a time yet in the future.

> Mat. 24:21 For then shall be great tribulation, such as was not since the beginning of the world to this time, no, nor ever shall be.
>
> Mat. 24:22 And except those days should be shortened, there should no flesh be saved: but for the elect's sake those days shall be shortened.

The Great Tribulation is going to be a time of great peril. Man will suffer persecution more than at any other time on earth; past, present, or future. Remember, there will be famines, pestilence, wars, earthquakes, antichrists, and forced worship. The Great Tribulation will be so severe that if God does not intervene, then no man would survive it.

God shortened the Great Tribulation to preserve man. The phrase *should be shortened*, mean to curtail, or impose restrictions. Please note, there is no reduction in the length of time of the Great Tribulation. It still lasted three and a half years. God shortens the Great Tribulation by restricting the amount of brutality that could be unleashed by the Antichrist. If God does not limit the application of cruelty that is distributed by the Antichrist, then every individual on the face of the earth will perish during the Great Tribulation.

Mat. 24:27   For as the lightning cometh out of the east, and shineth even unto the west; so shall also the coming of the Son of man be.

Mat. 24:28   For wheresoever the carcase is, there will the eagles be gathered together.

Jesus made it clear that during the Great Tribulation, there will be antichrists. Under no circumstances are men to go looking for Christ because all they will find are Antichrists. Seeking and honoring a false god is equivalent to worshipping the dead. Jesus referred to birds of prey gathering together. What do vultures do? To sustain their life, they go out to seek dead animals for food. Once they find the dead, they all congregate around it and eat until their heart is content. Mind you, this meal only provides temporary life support. God promised the saints eternal life. They must partake in that spiritual food supplied by Christ, who is alive and not dead. Christ also said that He would one day return for His saints, so there is no need for the saints to travel from place to place seeking Him. He will find all of His saints and *gather* them when He returns.

Jesus also told the disciples the manner of His return. He said He would come from the east, just like the rising of the sun. As one sees the sunrise in the east, he will also see Christ when He returns from the east. Revelation 1:7 states, "He cometh with clouds; and every eye shall see him, and they also which pierced him."

The second question the disciples asked Jesus was: what shall be the sign of His coming? The answer to the second question is, a time of Great Tribulation will begin immediately after the inauguration of the Abomination of Desolation. The Great Tribulation will be the sign that Christ will be returning soon. The Great Tribulation will be the worst time on earth ever, and *it will precede* Christ's return.

What Shall Be the End of the World?

Mat. 24:29   Immediately after the tribulation of those days shall the sun be darkened, and the moon shall not give her light, and the stars shall fall from heaven, and the powers of the heavens shall be shaken:

Mat. 24:30   And then shall appear the sign of the Son of man in heaven: and then shall all the tribes of the earth mourn, and they shall see the Son of man coming in the clouds of heaven with power and great glory.

Mat. 24:31   And he shall send his angels with a great sound of a trumpet, and they shall gather together his elect from the four winds, from one end of heaven to the other.

Jesus gives a definite time and season when He would return for His saints. He did not provide a date because no one knows the day or the hour, except God Himself. Matthew 24:36 states, "Of that day and hour knoweth no man, no, not the angels of heaven, but my Father only." Jesus did reveal to the disciples the season of His return. Luke 21:28 states, "When these things begin to come to pass, then look up, and lift up your heads; for your redemption draweth nigh." The things coming to pass that Jesus mentioned is famines, pestilences, earthquakes, tribulation, etc. Jesus narrowed down the timing of His return to be after the Great Tribulation. After the Tribulation, the heavens will undergo some traumatic changes. The Lord will darken the sun, the moon shall not give her light, many stars will fall from heaven, and the powers of the heavens will be agitated. Man will witness some events in the sky that have never previously existed. The natural order of the sky being disturbed is one sign that Christ is about to return for His saints.

Jesus continues by outlining the order in which the End-time events will occur. He stated that immediately after the Tribulation Period, He would modify the heavens. Then man will see Jesus coming in the clouds. Next, there would be the sound of a trumpet, and finally, He would gather all of His saints from the face of the earth.

The phrase used to describe the gathering together of the saints is another point of controversy. There's no doubt, His return is a glorious event, but many contend it to be the *Rapture*.

Some argue that it is the *Second Coming*. Still, others maintain this magnificent event to be the *First Resurrection*. Please note, the word *Rapture* and the phrase *Second Coming* does not appear in the KJV of the Bible. The term *First Resurrection* is the only one of the three most commonly used idioms to describe Christ's return that appears in the KJV of the Bible.

Rev. 20:4   And I saw thrones, and they sat upon them, and judgment was given unto them: and *I saw* the souls of them that were beheaded for the witness of Jesus, and for the word of God, and which had not worshipped the beast, neither his image, neither had received *his* mark upon their foreheads, or in their hands; and they lived and reigned with Christ a thousand years.

Rev. 20:5   But the rest of the dead lived not again until the thousand years were finished. This *is* the first resurrection.

Revelation 20:4-5 states that the *First Resurrection* will not occur until after the Antichrist implements the *Mark of the Beast*. The resurrection of the righteous individuals that had previously died will not happen until after the Great Tribulation. The text also states that this event is the First Resurrection. These verses eliminate the two-stage theory of Christ's return, known as the Rapture and the Second Coming, because it is impossible to have two (2) First Resurrections. You cannot have *the Rapture* and a *Second Coming* if the *First Resurrection* occurs after the Mark of the Beast's initiation.

Mat. 24:29   Immediately after the tribulation of those days shall the sun be darkened, and the moon shall not give her light, and the stars shall fall from heaven, and the powers of the heavens shall be shaken:

Mat. 24:30   And then shall appear the sign of the Son of man in heaven: and then shall all the tribes of the earth mourn, and they shall see the Son of man coming in the clouds of heaven with power and great glory.

Mat. 24:31   And he shall send his angels with a great sound of a trumpet, and they shall gather together his elect from the four winds, from one end of heaven to the other.

The use of the word *Rapture* is correct so long as there are no time restraints attached to it, such as Pre-Tribulation, Mid-Tribulation, or Post-Tribulation. The phrase *Second Coming* is a better choice because it is the second time that Christ will come to earth strictly for man's salvation. The term *First Resurrection* is the best choice because it entails that there cannot be any other resurrections before this one. Again, there cannot be two (2) First Resurrections.

When referencing Rapture and Second Coming, the implication is that *the Rapture* and *Second Coming* are two separate events. The phrase, *First Resurrection* disputes that claim. There cannot be *the Rapture*, which is a resurrection, and a *Second Coming*, which is a resurrection, unless they are co-occurring. The phrase, *First Resurrection*, clearly identifies *the Rapture* and the *Second Coming* to be synonymous.

The third question the disciples asked Jesus was: what shall be the sign of the end of the world? The answer to the third question is: there will be unimaginable changes in the sky. The Lord will darken the sun, the moon will refuse to shine, and the stars will move out of their assigned positions.

Comparisons of Christ's Return

1Th. 4:16   For the Lord himself shall descend from heaven with a shout, with the voice of the archangel, and with the trump of God: and the dead in Christ shall rise first:

1Th. 4:17   Then we which are alive *and* remain shall be caught up together with them in the clouds, to meet the Lord in the air: and so shall we ever be with the Lord.

Mat. 24:29   Immediately after the tribulation of those days shall the sun be darkened, and the moon shall not give her light, and the stars shall fall from heaven, and the powers of the heavens shall be shaken:

Mat. 24:30   And then shall appear the sign of the Son of man in heaven: and then shall all the tribes of the earth mourn, and they shall see the Son of man coming in the clouds of heaven with power and great glory.

Mat. 24:31   And he shall send his angels with a great sound of a trumpet, and they shall gather together his elect from the four winds, from one end of heaven to the other.

When comparing the account of Christ's return by Paul in 1 Thessalonians with the description given by Jesus in Matthew 24, we see that both reports are similar. Both versions mention Christ returning in the clouds, the sounding of a trump or trumpet, the presence of angels or archangels, which are heavenly beings. Both accounts also address the *gathering together* of the saints. It is fair to conclude that both interpretations of these events are synonymous. The only difference between the two accounts of His return is that in Jesus' version, it will take place immediately after the Tribulation, and Paul's writings do not give any reference at all concerning the actual timing of Christ's return. Considering both men's authority, not to diminish Paul's impeccable writing, one must allude to identify with Jesus' account, concerning His return. We take this stand only because of Jesus' relationship with God, the Father who knows all things. Jesus' version imparts more information, thereby giving us a more accurate picture and understanding of how and when Christ will return.

CHAPTER 3

THE TRIBULATION PERIOD

Mat. 24:21   For then shall be great tribulation, such as was not since the beginning of the world to this time, no, nor ever shall be.

1Th. 4:17   Then we which are alive *and* remain shall be caught up together with them in the clouds, to meet the Lord in the air: and so shall we ever be with the Lord.

Mat. 24:31   And he shall send his angels with a great sound of a trumpet, and they shall gather together his elect from the four winds, from one end of heaven to the other.

Rev. 20:5   But the rest of the dead lived not again until the thousand years were finished. This *is* the first resurrection.

WHENEVER we mention the Tribulation Period; these phrases always come to mind, *the Rapture and the Second Coming*. Neither one of these phrases appears in the KJV. The implication is that the Bible references the Rapture and Second Coming with two expressions. 1Thessalonians 4:17 uses the term *caught up together*. Matthew 24:31 refers to it as *the gathering together*. There is another phrase that is hardly ever mentioned. Revelation 20:5 clearly define and name this event as *the First Resurrection*. All three of these scriptures describe the saints' resurrection, but the phrase *First Resurrection* takes it a step further. It distinguishes the timing of its occurrence. By identifying this event as the *First Resurrection*, it signifies that no resurrection precedes it. This fact indicates that the First Resurrection, Rapture, and Second Coming are synonymous.

As we endeavor to entirely grasp the Tribulation Period's dynamics, we must ask a series of questions. The answer to these questions will reveal a more vivid understanding of such an important event.

- What is the Tribulation Period?
- When will the Tribulation Period begin?
- What is the Abomination of Desolation?
- Will man be allowed to shop for groceries?
- What is the purpose of the Great Tribulation?
- What are the different Tribulation viewpoints?
- The Tribulation and the Wrath, are they synonymous?

What is the Tribulation Period?

The word *tribulation* means pressure, trouble, anguish, and persecution. To paint a more vivid picture of the Tribulation, let's describe it as severe mental and physical suffering caused by the exertion of continuous force to persuade someone to do something against his or her will. This description pretty much sums up the typical livelihood and severity of human agony experienced during the Tribulation Period.

> Mat. 24:21   For then shall be great tribulation, such as was not since the beginning of the world to this time, no, nor ever shall be.

Note, this tribulation is not just the daily challenges that accompany life in general; this is the *Great Tribulation*. That means that its application will be at an elevated level of intensity for an extended period. Scripture describes the Great Tribulation as a time of trouble on earth that is worse than it has ever been or ever will be.

When will the Tribulation Period Begin?

Dan. 9:24   Seventy weeks are determined upon thy people
and upon thy holy city, to finish the transgression,
and to make an end of sins, and to make
reconciliation for iniquity, and to bring in
everlasting righteousness, and to seal up the
vision and prophecy, and to anoint the most
Holy.

Dan. 9:25   Know therefore and understand, *that* from the
going forth of the commandment to restore and
to build Jerusalem unto the Messiah the Prince
shall be seven weeks, and threescore and two
weeks: the street shall be built again, and the wall,
even in troublous times.

Dan. 9:26   And after threescore and two weeks shall Messiah
be cut off, but not for himself: and the people of
the prince that shall come shall destroy the city
and the sanctuary; and the end thereof *shall be*
with a flood, and unto the end of the war
desolations are determined.

To understand the actual beginning of the Tribulation Period,
we have to journey to the book of Daniel in the Old Testament.
Daniel was in exile in Babylon when he received this prophecy.
Gabriel, the archangel, proclaimed to Daniel that the holy city,
Jerusalem, will endure 70 weeks of troublous times. The word *week*
is a Hebrew word that means *seven*. Although it only means *seven,*
its application is widespread. It could be seven seconds, seven days,
seven years, seven centuries, etc. The actual meaning will have to
be determined by the contents of the text. In this case, it means
seven years because it is directly related to events that have already
taken place in history. It is referencing the rebuilding of the temple
in Jerusalem and the death of the Messiah.

Daniel stated that there is a total of 70 weeks to finish the
transgression of Jerusalem. The 70 weeks equals 70 weeks of years
($7 * 70 = 490$) years. The king gave the commandment to rebuild
the temple, and it took seven weeks ($7 * 7$) or 49 years before the
temple's completion. Once the temple was completed and

dedicated, another sixty-two weeks (7 * 62) or 434 years passed before the Messiah's death. The addition of 49 years and 434 years equals 483 years. That leaves *one week* that is unaccountable. Four hundred ninety years minus four hundred eighty-three years have a remainder of seven years or one week.

Christ's death on the cross was the end of the Old Testament and the beginning of the New Testament. Jesus' death was also the beginning of a new era, known as *the Times of the Gentiles, or* the grafting of the gentiles into the olive tree or covenant of Israel. Meaning there was a break in time between the 69th and 70th week of Daniel's prophecy. Once *the Times of the Gentiles* is complete, then and only then will God turn His attention; back to Jerusalem. That will be the beginning of the one (1) remaining *week* or seven years. The classification of that final week is the Tribulation Period, and the book of Revelation provides extraordinary details.

> Dan. 9:27   And he shall confirm the covenant with many for one week: and in the midst of the week he shall cause the sacrifice and the oblation to cease, and for the overspreading of abominations he shall make *it* desolate, even until the consummation, and that determined shall be poured upon the desolate.

The book of Daniel confirms that the *Tribulation Period* is the final seven years that God will deal with Jerusalem. During that time, a man known as the Antichrist will surface. He will establish a seven-year covenant with the nation of Israel. This seven-year covenant coincides with the Tribulation Period. Approximately three and a half years into that seven-year covenant, the Antichrist will deliberately violate the covenant by declaring that Israel can no longer continue their daily sacrifices. At that time, Antichrist will assume control of the temple. Daniel 8:11 states, "And the place of his sanctuary was cast down." Soon after the daily sacrifice is prohibited, the Antichrist will then implement *the Abomination of Desolation.* Daniel 11:31 states, "And they shall pollute the sanctuary of strength, and shall take away the daily sacrifice, and they shall place the abomination that maketh desolate." Once the Abomination of Desolation is in place, the Great Tribulation will begin. Matthew 24:15-21 states, "When ye therefore shall see the abomination of desolation, spoken of by Daniel the prophet ... let them which be in Judaea flee ... then shall be great tribulation." The Tribulation Period is seven years, but *the Great Tribulation* will last for approximately three and a half years. The Tribulation Period will begin when the Antichrist signs a seven-year covenant with the nation of Israel. Still, the Great Tribulation will not start until the last half of that seven-year covenant.

What is the Abomination of Desolation?

Antichrist establishes the Abomination of Desolation. He will ban the nation of Israel from their daily sacrifices of worshipping their God. He will show himself to be God, and he will demand that the Hebrew people worship him as such. The followers of Antichrist will place a statue or image in the likeness of Antichrist at the holy site in Jerusalem. They strategically placed the figure so the people can worship it as the one and only God. This image is *the Abomination of Desolation.* Abomination is something that Almighty God utterly abhors. Desolation is destruction; therefore, the Abomination of Desolation is an act so horrible that it leads to eternal damnation. Worshipping an image of a false God as Almighty God is the Abomination of Desolation. The result of worshipping this image is the loss of salvation, which leads to the eternal destruction of the soul.

> Rev. 13:16 And he causeth all, both small and great, rich and poor, free and bond, to receive a mark in their right hand, or in their foreheads:
> Rev. 13:17 And that no man might buy or sell, save he that had the mark, or the name of the beast, or the number of his name.

The Abomination of Desolation is associated with the *Mark of the Beast.* A common belief is that the Mark of the Beast is 666, but that's not necessarily so. The Mark of the Beast could be any one of three different things. It can be a mark, the name of the beast, or the number of his name. Yes, it could be 666, which is the number that symbolizes his name. It could be a mark or symbol that represents his name. It could also be his very name. Regardless, whether it is a name, number, or mark, all of them are blasphemous. Worshipping anyone of them will result in an individual losing his soul forever.

> Rev. 14:9   And the third angel followed them, saying with a loud voice, If any man worship the beast and his image, and receive *his* mark in his forehead, or in his hand,
>
> Rev. 14:10 The same shall drink of the wine of the wrath of God, which is poured out without mixture into the cup of his indignation; and he shall be tormented with fire and brimstone in the presence of the holy angels, and in the presence of the Lamb:
>
> Rev. 14:11 And the smoke of their torment ascendeth up for ever and ever: and they have no rest day nor night, who worship the beast and his image, and whosoever receiveth the mark of his name.

Not only will an individual lose his or her soul if he accepts the mark, the name, or the number of his name. An individual can also lose his or her soul if they even worships the beast. Worshipping the beast or accepting his mark, his name, or his number is *Blasphemy of the Holy Spirit,* of which there is no repentance. Blasphemy of the Holy Spirit will result in an individual's damnation forever. Matthew 12:32 states, "Whosoever speaketh against the Holy Ghost, it shall not be forgiven him, neither in this world, neither in the world to come."

Will Man Be Allowed to Shop for Groceries?

> Rev. 13:17 And that no man might buy or sell, save he that had the mark, or the name of the beast, or the number of his name.

Most people associate the *Great Tribulation Period* with buying and selling. The *buying and selling* in this text aren't referencing purchasing the necessities of life, such as food and clothing. It is referencing *buying and selling* on a much grander scale. It's talking about becoming a merchant that buys and sells for a profit. The entire chapter of Revelation 18 focuses on the fall of Babylon, which is Antichrist's kingdom. Notice who the people are that are weeping and wailing. It is only the merchants that are mourning. These are the individuals allowed *to buy and sell* on a corporate level, only because they took the *Mark of the Beast*. Buying and selling in the Revelation chapter 13 is not a reference to grocery shopping.

What is the Purpose of the Great Tribulation?

Rev. 12:7   And there was war in heaven: Michael and his angels fought against the dragon; and the dragon fought and his angels,

Rev. 12:8   And prevailed not; neither was their place found any more in heaven.

Rev. 12:9   And the great dragon was cast out, that old serpent, called the Devil, and Satan, which deceiveth the whole world: he was cast out into the earth, and his angels were cast out with him.

Rev. 12:10   And I heard a loud voice saying in heaven, Now is come salvation, and strength, and the kingdom of our God, and the power of his Christ: for the accuser of our brethren is cast down, which accused them before our God day and night.

Rev. 12:11   And they overcame him by the blood of the Lamb, and by the word of their testimony; and they loved not their lives unto the death.

Rev. 12:12   Therefore rejoice, *ye* heavens, and ye that dwell in them. Woe to the inhabiters of the earth and of the sea! for the devil is come down unto you, having great wrath, because he knoweth that he hath but a short time.

During the Tribulation Period, there will be many significant wars on earth and in heaven. Michael, the archangel, and his angels will engage Satan and his angels. Ultimately, Satan and his angels are going to lose the war. As a result of losing the battle, The Lord expels them from heaven. With no other place to reside, they relocate on earth. Satan instantly recognizes the permanent revocation of his heavenly privileges. Then he will realize that he only has a short time before he will be confined and tormented in the Bottomless Pit. Remember that adage; *misery loves company?* To ensure that he doesn't get lonely, Satan will launch a massive assault on the earth's inhabitants. 1 Peter 5:8 states, "Your adversary the devil, as a roaring lion, walketh about, seeking whom he may devour." The Devil's final push to destroy innocent individuals is the beginning of *the Great Tribulation.* His purpose is to ruin as many souls as possible before the return of Christ.

What are the Different Tribulation Viewpoints

There are three main viewpoints concerning the timing of the return of Christ for His saints. Those viewpoints are *Pre-Tribulation, Mid-Tribulation, and Post-Tribulation.*

Those that believe in the Pre-Tribulation Theory, believe that Christ will return before the Tribulation Period begins. Christ will come back and gather together the saints in the air and return to heaven until the Tribulation Period end seven years later. After the Tribulation Period, Christ will return to earth with the saints to establish His Millennial kingdom.

The Mid-Tribulation Theory is very similar to the Pre-Tribulation view. The only difference is that Christ will return sometime around the middle of the Tribulation Period. He will gather together the saints in the air and return to heaven until the Tribulation Period ends, three and a half years later. After the Tribulation Period, Christ will return to earth with the saints to establish His Millennial kingdom.

The Post-Tribulation Theory is entirely different from the Pre-Tribulation and Mid-Tribulation theories. It is a belief that Christ will return to gather the saints at the end of the Tribulation

Period, meaning the saints will have to endure the entire Tribulation Period. Once He returns to collect the saints in the air, He will immediately return to earth with the saints to establish His Millennial kingdom.

Tribulation and Wrath are not Synonymous

Tribulation is severe mental and physical suffering caused by the exertion of continuous force to persuade someone to do something against his or her will. *Wrath* is vengeance or justifiable punishment for a deliberate offense that is utterly repulsive and disgusting. The result of both Tribulation and Wrath is pain and suffering, but what separates or distinguishes the difference between the two are the underlying reasons for experiencing that pain and suffering. Man, as a means of persuasion, applies Tribulation so that one will adhere to his intended plan. On the other hand, God administers His Wrath, which is just punishment for totally disrespecting His laws by following Satan.

Rev. 12:9   And the great dragon was cast out, that old serpent, called the Devil, and Satan, which deceiveth the whole world: he was cast out into the earth, and his angels were cast out with him.

Rev. 12:12   Therefore rejoice, *ye* heavens, and ye that dwell in them. Woe to the inhabiters of the earth and of the sea! for the devil is come down unto you, having great wrath, because he knoweth that he hath but a short time.

Rev. 12:13   And when the dragon saw that he was cast unto the earth, he persecuted the woman which brought forth the man *child*.

Who or what is the motivating force that causes an individual to experience Tribulation? It is Satan. He receives permanent expulsion from heaven to earth, and the heavens are rejoicing because of his departure. On the other hand, the inhabitants on earth will experience misery and turmoil, better known as *Tribulation.*

Satan is a spiritual being and operates in an invisible or spiritual realm. He has targeted the inhabitants of the earth, which lives in the physical earth. He needs a willing human being who can operate in the physical realm to bring his evil desires. He finds a man with similar ambitions, so he entices him to become his accomplice. That man will become known as the Antichrist.

Why is Satan using the Antichrist to distribute Tribulation upon the earth's inhabitants? Satan initiates trials and hardship because it's apparent that he has only a short time before he will undoubtedly face the Wrath or justifiable punishment that he so deserves. And he wants as much company as possible to join him in this fate.

The human race experiences setbacks and hardship every day of their life, so it's safe to say that *Tribulation* is already on earth. Still, it will escalate during the actual Tribulation Period. It will begin to peak in the middle of the Tribulation Period when Satan finds himself expelled from heaven. At that time, Tribulation becomes the Great Tribulation.

> Rom. 1:18   For the wrath of God is revealed from heaven against all ungodliness and unrighteousness of men, who hold the truth in unrighteousness;

> Joh. 3:36   He that believeth on the Son hath everlasting life: and he that believeth not the Son shall not see life; but the wrath of God abideth on him.

We have seen that man cannot escape from being a victim of the Devil's Tribulation. 1 Peter 5:8 states, "Your adversary the devil, as a roaring lion, walketh about, seeking whom he may devour." The Devil does not discriminate; no one is immune from Tribulation. He plans to recruit as many people as possible to join his social party of ungodliness and unrighteousness. This social gathering will be one hot party, pun intended.

> 1Th. 5:9   For God hath not appointed us to wrath, but to obtain salvation by our Lord Jesus Christ,

Even though man does not choose whether or not he has a part in the Tribulation, he does have a choice whether or not he participates in the Wrath. Satan administers Tribulation on the human race. God dispenses Wrath to all men that live ungodly lives. Choose to repent and receive salvation or choose not to repent and accept the Wrath of God.

God desires not to lose even one soul. 2 Peter 3:9 states, "But is longsuffering to us-ward, not willing that any should perish, but that all should come to repentance." For that reason, God sent His Son Jesus Christ into the world to die for our sins. Joh. 3:16 states, "God so loved the world, that he gave his only begotten Son, that whosoever believeth in him should not perish, but have everlasting life."

There is much confusion concerning Tribulation and Wrath. Some think that it is just two ways to say the same thing. The difference is, Satan administers Tribulation by his man, the Antichrist, and God applies His Wrath by His angels. Again, man enforces Tribulation, and God delivers the Wrath. The weapon Satan uses to keep an individual from repenting is Tribulation. God administers His Wrath as punishment to those individuals that refuse to obey His word.

CHAPTER 4

THE WRATH OF GOD

Mat. 24:29 Immediately after the tribulation of those days shall the sun be darkened, and the moon shall not give her light, and the stars shall fall from heaven, and the powers of the heavens shall be shaken:

Mat. 24:30 And then shall appear the sign of the Son of man in heaven: and then shall all the tribes of the earth mourn, and they shall see the Son of man coming in the clouds of heaven with power and great glory.

Mat. 24:31 And he shall send his angels with a great sound of a trumpet, and they shall gather together his elect from the four winds, from one end of heaven to the other.

THE Millennium cannot take place until after the seven years Tribulation is complete. Matthew 24:29-31 clearly shows that Christ does not return to gather His saints until immediately after the Tribulation. The gathering of the saints is a necessary step that ushers in the everlasting kingdom. The first thousand years of the eternal kingdom is known as the Millennium. This name is appropriate because one thousand years is *a Millennium,* just as ten years is a decade, and one hundred years is a century. The period between the Tribulation's end and the Millennium's beginning is the focal point of this chapter.

This book addresses this period because there is widespread confusion concerning the Tribulation and the Wrath. Often, one will refer to the events taking place during the Tribulation Period as God's Wrath. No, the Tribulation is a time of extreme trouble implemented on earth just before the return of Christ. Satan influences this Tribulation, and an individual known as the Antichrist orchestrates it. On the other hand, God ultimately initiates and directs His Wrath at the conclusion of the Tribulation Period.

The Wrath of God should not be confused with the Tribulation of man. Tribulation is initiated by man, which is systematic acts of mental and physical abuse to persuade men and women to rethink his or her position on God. On the other hand, God initiates His Wrath, which is the just punishment that God administers on those who refused to implement the Word of God in their everyday lives. Tribulation comes before the return of Christ, and God's Wrath comes immediately after His return.

Famine, pestilences, rationing, and restrictions on religious worship will be the weapons of choice used to administer the Tribulation upon man. These tools will be systematically initiated and monitored during the Tribulation Period. Invariably, the powers that be will enact new laws to maximize the most significant amount of fear, pain, and suffering. Restricting life necessities, such as food, clothing, and shelter reduces one to a beggar. Compounding that mental state, along with forced worship of a God not of one's choosing, reduces that individual to a state of complete worthlessness. Such a person possesses nothing, not even his soul.

God will administer His Wrath in a series of events called the outpouring of the Vials of Wrath. There are a total of seven vials that God pours out in succession. The outpouring of these vials is a harsh punishment, and it gets progressively worse with the outpouring of each one. This punishment is severe and permanent because it is called the seven last plagues. God's Wrath is the ultimate punishment, and among its intended targets, there are no survivors.

The First Vial

Rev. 16:2   And the first went, and poured out his vial upon the earth; and there fell a noisome and grievous sore upon the men which had the mark of the beast, and *upon* them which worshipped his image.

The first angel will pour his vial upon the earth. Everyone that had accepted the mark of the beast immediately received a horrible sore upon his or her body. This punishment is the first of several Vials of Wrath that will affect all individuals who worshiped the beast as their God or accepted his identifying mark, commonly known as the Mark of the Beast (666).

The Second Vial

> Rev. 16:3   And the second angel poured out his vial upon the sea; and it became as the blood of a dead *man*: and every living soul died in the sea.

The second angel will follow the lead of the first angel by pouring out his vial. Unlike the first vial that's poured upon the earth, the angel spurts the second vial into the sea. When the vial contents touched the water, immediately, the water's consistency changed from a thin liquid to a thick coagulated substance. The transformation of the water caused it to be stagnated and can no longer flow freely. All sea life dies as a result of pouring out the second vial upon the sea.

The Third Vial

> Rev. 16:4   And the third angel poured out his vial upon the rivers and fountains of waters; and they became blood.
>
> Rev. 16:5   And I heard the angel of the waters say, Thou art righteous, O Lord, which art, and wast, and shalt be, because thou hast judged thus.
>
> Rev. 16:6   For they have shed the blood of saints and prophets, and thou hast given them blood to drink; for they are worthy.
>
> Rev. 16:7   And I heard another out of the altar say, Even so, Lord God Almighty, true and righteous *are* thy judgments.

The third angel pours the third vial upon the rivers and streams. Just as the seawater became stagnated when the angel introduced the second vial's contents, the rivers and streams will also become useless. When the rivers and streams become contaminated, it will pollute the supply of drinking water.

The angels will begin to comment on the catastrophes that will be plaguing the earth. They will be confirming this punishment to be just and that God is merely ridding the world of all unrighteousness.

The Fourth Vial

> Rev. 16:8   And the fourth angel poured out his vial upon the sun; and power was given unto him to scorch men with fire.
>
> Rev. 16:9   And men were scorched with great heat, and blasphemed the name of God, which hath power over these plagues: and they repented not to give him glory.

The fourth angel will pour his vial upon the sun. The contents of the fourth vial react with the sun and cause intensification of the sun's rays. The heat from the sun will be so severe that it will produce a severe case of sunburn. Even while suffering severe pain, from the sunburn, sores, and lack of water to cool their tongues, the recipients continue to blaspheme Almighty God. Remember, the individuals experiencing these awful plagues are the ones that accepted the Mark of the Beast. By taking the Mark of the Beast, one denies Almighty God and adopts the Antichrist as their God. Because of their blasphemous attitude, they attribute their pain and agony to an evil spirit, fighting against their god. They do not realize they are receiving their just punishment for rejecting Almighty God. The question becomes, why won't their God (Antichrist) come to their aid and comfort them. The answer is, their God (Antichrist) is powerless against Almighty God.

The Fifth Vial

Rev. 16:10   And the fifth angel poured out his vial upon the seat of the beast; and his kingdom was full of darkness; and they gnawed their tongues for pain,

Rev. 16:11   And blasphemed the God of heaven because of their pains and their sores, and repented not of their deeds.

An angel pours the fifth vial's contents on the headquarters or capital of the Antichrist's kingdom. Antichrist's kingdom becomes darkened, and his followers become blind with the outpouring of the fifth vial. It's not only their eyes that are blind; their hearts and minds lack Godly wisdom also. They are experiencing enormous tragedy, extreme pain, and unbearable suffering, but they refuse to connect the dots. Satan, the God whom they serve, isn't doing anything to comfort them, but they continue to give him praise while they curse Almighty God.

The Sixth Vial

Rev. 16:12   And the sixth angel poured out his vial upon the great river Euphrates; and the water thereof was dried up, that the way of the kings of the east might be prepared.

Rev. 16:13   And I saw three unclean spirits like frogs *come* out of the mouth of the dragon, and out of the mouth of the beast, and out of the mouth of the false prophet.

Rev. 16:14   For they are the spirits of devils, working miracles, *which* go forth unto the kings of the earth and of the whole world, to gather them to the battle of that great day of God Almighty.

Rev. 16:15   Behold, I come as a thief. Blessed *is* he that watcheth, and keepeth his garments, lest he walk naked, and they see his shame.

Rev. 16:16   And he gathered them together into a place called in the Hebrew tongue Armageddon.

When the sixth angel pours his vial upon the Euphrates River, the waters of the river will dry up. This massive drought situation produces a dry riverbed, to be utilized as a highway for transporting armies and supplies from the east.

John, the writer of the book of Revelation, also witnessed the interaction of unclean spirits. Remember, John is having an out-of-body experience, and he's observing spiritual things. He saw three unclean spirits come out of the mouth of Satan, out of the mouth of Antichrist, and out of the mouth of the False Prophet. They have the appearance of frogs that hop from one individual to another to influence them to participate in the Battle of Armageddon. They are aligning themselves to fight against Almighty God. The Battle of Armageddon is the last war before Jesus establishes His everlasting kingdom on earth.

John was giving another warning when he stated that Jesus would be coming as a thief. He's confirming that no one knows the day or the hour, but the human race should prepare themselves so that the Lord does not find them living in an un-repented state. The implication is that if one does not endure or obey the Word of God to the end, then it will not be a pleasant encounter when Christ returns. One does not want to be confederate against Christ at the Battle of Armageddon.

The Seventh Vial

Rev. 16:17   And the seventh angel poured out his vial into the air; and there came a great voice out of the temple of heaven, from the throne, saying, It is done.

Rev. 16:18   And there were voices, and thunders, and lightnings; and there was a great earthquake, such as was not since men were upon the earth, so mighty an earthquake, *and* so great.

Rev. 16:19   And the great city was divided into three parts, and the cities of the nations fell: and great Babylon came in remembrance before God, to give unto her the cup of the wine of the fierceness of his wrath.

Rev. 16:20   And every island fled away, and the mountains were not found.

Rev. 16:21   And there fell upon men a great hail out of heaven, *every stone* about the weight of a talent: and men blasphemed God because of the plague of the hail; for the plague thereof was exceeding great.

The outpouring of the seventh and final vial is the culmination of the fierceness of Almighty God's Wrath. The angel pours the seventh vial into the air. The purpose of this vial is to destroy the spirit that works in the children of disobedience. Ephesians 2:2 states, "Wherein in time past ye walked according to the course of this world, according to the prince of the power of the air, the spirit that now worketh in the children of disobedience."

When the angel pours the seventh vial into the air, the earth will undergo extraordinary growing pains. The most significant earthquake ever recorded will occur, causing cities to be divided and swallowed up. The mountains and islands will shun away from the one sitting on the throne. The most massive hailstones ever recorded will fall from the sky and crush men to death.

The above events are the reformation of the earth. This transformation is known as the new heaven and new earth. Revelation 21:1 states, "I saw a new heaven and a new earth: for the first heaven and the first earth were passed away." Sometimes, the destruction of this world is a foregone conclusion that God replaces this present earth with another one. No, God will never destroy this present earth; it will be here forever. When the angel pours the final vial into the air, it will modify the heavens and triggers a series of events that will displace mountains, islands, oceans, etc. The earth will undergo a major remodeling to change its appearance, but God will never destroy this present earth. Ecclesiastes 1:4 states, "*One* generation passeth away, and *another* generation cometh: but the earth abideth for ever."

With the outpouring of the seventh vial into the air, the kingdoms of this present world become extinct forever. Man will no longer be the ruler of this world. When the voice comes from heaven, stating, "*it is done,*" this will be the end of this present world, as we know it and the beginning of the everlasting kingdom that God promised us so many years ago.

The angels pour out the Wrath of God in seven successive vials. The angels pour them upon the land, air, and the seas. Virtually, man's entire environment will be affected by these seven Vials of Wrath. It is God's way of dispelling all unrighteousness and ushering in a world free of Satan's evil influence.

> Zec. 3:9   For behold the stone that I have laid before Joshua; upon one stone *shall be* seven eyes: behold, I will engrave the graving thereof, saith the LORD of hosts, and I will remove the iniquity of that land in one day.

> Rev. 18:8   Therefore shall her plagues come in one day, death, and mourning, and famine; and she shall be utterly burned with fire: for strong *is* the Lord God who judgeth her.

The outpouring of the seven vials that shows the fierceness of the Wrath of God will not be a long, drawn out process. God's Wrath will be dispensed in a short time, perhaps one twenty-four-hour period. Unlike man's Tribulation that lasts for seven years, God's Wrath will only last for approximately one day. Maybe it takes even less time than twenty-four hours to pour out the seven vials. Revelation 18:10 states, "For in one hour is thy judgment come."

> Rev. 16:2   And the first went, and poured out his vial upon the earth; and there fell a noisome and grievous sore upon the men which had the mark of the beast, and *upon* them which worshipped his image.

The Tribulation administered by man will not discriminate. Antichrist dispenses it upon all men. The Wrath of God is different. It is very biased and precise. It is the just punishment for only those that openly rejected Almighty God and accepted the Antichrist as their God. Unlike parents that sometimes punish all their children for assurance that the guilty child does not go unpunished, God's Wrath is quite discriminating. His Wrath only affects those that are guilty.

CHAPTER 5

THE MARK OF THE BEAST

THE *Mark of the Beast* is one of those topics that raise the eyebrows of many. Quite often, it is associated with the notion that the number 666 is the number of death. People often do not want to accept their change from a purchase if it totals $6.66. Most people think that everyone living during the Tribulation Period will have to either get the *Mark of the Beast* or face execution.

The phrase, *Mark of the Beast,* originated in Revelation, chapter 13. Because the idiom originated from two essential words, *mark* and *beast,* let's isolate each word to get a broader perspective of its meaning. We will start with the word *beast.* What exactly does the term *beast,* in that phrase, mean? Is this beast an animal, such as a wolf, or is it something else, that's a little more sinister?

Rev. 13:1   And I stood upon the sand of the sea, and saw a beast rise up out of the sea, having seven heads and ten horns, and upon his horns ten crowns, and upon his heads the name of blasphemy.

Rev. 13:2   And the beast which I saw was like unto a leopard, and his feet were as *the feet* of a bear, and his mouth as the mouth of a lion: and the dragon gave him his power, and his seat, and great authority.

The Beast Rising Out of the Sea

In Revelation chapter 13, John is describing a beast that rose out of the sea. This beast had the appearance of a leopard with a bear's feet, and it spoke with the mouth of a lion. Not only did the creature look like three different animals, but it also possessed seven-heads, ten horns, and ten crowns. None of the before mentioned animals have horns nor crowns. Because of all these anatomical discrepancies, it is a good possibility the beast is not an

animal but a replica of something else. Note, the book of
Revelation is a book of symbolism.

Dan. 7:1	In the first year of Belshazzar king of Babylon Daniel had a dream and visions of his head upon his bed: then he wrote the dream, *and* told the sum of the matters.
Dan. 7:2	Daniel spake and said, I saw in my vision by night, and, behold, the four winds of the heaven strove upon the great sea.
Dan. 7:3	And four great beasts came up from the sea, diverse one from another.
Dan. 7:4	The first *was* like a lion, and had eagle's wings: I beheld till the wings thereof were plucked, and it was lifted up from the earth, and made stand upon the feet as a man, and a man's heart was given to it.
Dan. 7:5	And behold another beast, a second, like to a bear, and it raised up itself on one side, and *it had* three ribs in the mouth of it between the teeth of it: and they said thus unto it, Arise, devour much flesh.
Dan. 7:6	After this I beheld, and lo another, like a leopard, which had upon the back of it four wings of a fowl; the beast had also four heads; and dominion was given to it.
Dan. 7:7	After this I saw in the night visions, and behold a fourth beast, dreadful and terrible, and strong exceedingly; and it had great iron teeth: it devoured and brake in pieces, and stamped the residue with the feet of it: and it *was* diverse from all the beasts that *were* before it; and it had ten horns.

The book of Revelation and the book of Daniel are books of
prophecy, and they mirror each other. In Daniel chapter 7, Daniel
witnessed four (4) formidable beasts rising from the sea. The first

three creatures resembled a lion, a bear, and a leopard, respectively. The one (1) beast that John saw in Revelation is a combination of the same animals that Daniel saw in his dream. The fourth beast that Daniel saw is dreadful and terrible. Note, it is an amalgamation of the first three beasts, but now it has grown ten horns. Upon closer examination, the creature that John witnessed in Revelation chapter 13 is the fourth beast that Daniel saw in Daniel chapter 7. Note the similarities between the four beasts that Daniel saw and the one creature that John witnessed.

- They come up out of the sea
- They consist of a lion, bear, and leopard
- They have ten horns

It's a foregone conclusion that both John and Daniel describe the same beast, but this beast is not an ordinary animal. This beast is something far more complex. One could only guess what this creature represents, but scripture provisioned us with this mysterious animal's exact identity.

Dan. 7:17   These great beasts, which are four, *are* four kings, *which* shall arise out of the earth.

Dan. 7:23   Thus he said, The fourth beast shall be the fourth kingdom upon earth, which shall be diverse from all kingdoms, and shall devour the whole earth, and shall tread it down, and break it in pieces.

The beasts are not animals at all; they are four different kings. Kingdoms are the territory that kings reign over; therefore, these *beasts* are symbolic for kingdoms. The fourth beast, described by Daniel, is the same beast described by John. It is the fourth kingdom, and it is the final earthly government, under the authority of human beings. Scripture goes on to tell us that the saints will inherit the fourth kingdom after its collapse.

Many have come to realize that the *beast* in the phrase *Mark of the Beast* is a kingdom. In the expression, Mark of the Beast, the next task is to isolate and identify the actual meaning of the word *mark*.

The definition of *mark* is an impression or inscription placed on the surface of an object. It can be a sign, a symbol, a brand, an image, a seal, or anything that identifies or denotes ownership. Some examples of a mark would be the king's signet ring, the presidential seal, the official seal certifying documents, etc. In conclusion, the phrase *Mark of the Beast* is an identifying brand or inscription. This brand designates the undisputed ownership of a powerful king or kingdom.

The foregone conclusion is that the Mark of the Beast represents an autocratic form of government. Many empires or kingdoms in the past have been dictatorships. There are still nations under a dictatorship today. It is conceivable to think that the realm identified by the Mark of the Beast has already passed because Daniel wrote about these events over 2500 years ago. Again, scripture provides the answers. Daniel 7:18 states, "The saints of the most High shall take the kingdom, and possess the kingdom for ever, even for ever and ever." We know that the saints are not the governing authority on earth at this particular time. Eventually, the saints of God will take possession of this kingdom. Therefore, one must conclude that this kingdom is the world's final kingdom, but this kingdom's birth is still future to us today. Upon establishing this kingdom, it will be under the authority of a man known as Antichrist, and this is an appropriate title because he will oppose God in every aspect.

Every government or kingdom has an official seal. The Mark of the Beast is the official seal of the Antichrist's kingdom. No government's seal has received more press than the Antichrist's official seal. Many people from all walks of life have conversed about the Mark of the Beast for centuries. There is something mysteriously significant about the Mark of the Beast. Never before have any government required its citizens to receive an official seal on their person. Some have even ventured to say, the Mark of the Beast will be a governmental chip implanted under the skin of individuals for identification purposes.

Rev. 13:16   And he causeth all, both small and great, rich and poor, free and bond, to receive a mark in their right hand, or in their foreheads:

Rev. 13:17   And that no man might buy or sell, save he that had the mark, or the name of the beast, or the number of his name.

Rev. 13:18   Here is wisdom. Let him that hath understanding count the number of the beast: for it is the number of a man; and his number *is* Six hundred threescore *and* six.

Acceptance of the Mark of the Beast

The *Mark of the Beast* has been one of the most talked-about prophetic subjects. Usually, it surfaces every time there is a discussion about the End-times. This topic is fear-driven because many believe it affects the entire population of the world socially, economically, and religiously. People must choose between accepting the Mark of the Beast or facing instant death. It is a time of final decision-making; not only for your life, but also for your soul.

In most circles, the Mark of the Beast is the number 666. The Mark of the Beast can be the number 666, but it can be more than just a number. Under closer scrutiny, the Mark of the Beast can be a mark, a name, or a number. Revelation 13:16-17 states, "And he causeth all, both small and great, rich and poor, free and bond, to receive a mark in their right hand, or in their foreheads: And that no man might buy or sell, save he that had the mark, or the name of the beast, or the number of his name."

By design, the Mark of the Beast has no limitations at all. Without question, most people understand that the *number 666* is significant to Antichrist, but what about his name or mark? Most people who study prophecy only allude to the number aspect of the phrase *Mark of the Beast* and not recognize the *mark* or the *name?*

Many individuals assume that the mark and number are identical. They seem to think that the number 666 is the number that will be marked or tattooed on the heads or hands of people living in Antichrist's kingdom. The Mark of the Beast can be any one of three things. It can be a number, which is accepted to be 666. It can be a mark, such as an identifying symbol. It can be a logo, which readily identifies ownership, such as a flag, brand, or trademark. These items can respectively correspond to a nation, product, or corporation. The Mark of the Beast can also be the name of the Antichrist's kingdom. Revelation 17:5 states, "Upon her forehead was a name written, MYSTERY, BABYLON THE GREAT, THE MOTHER OF HARLOTS AND ABOMINATIONS OF THE EARTH." This name is too long to be stamped on someone's forehead; therefore, it is conceivable to think they will condense this name into a much smaller mark or emblem, but with the same meaning. That being the case, the name, the mark, or the number are synonymous because either form represents the beast.

The Mark's Association with Buying and Selling

Another fear factor associated with the Mark of the Beast is *buying and selling*. Many have stated that it will be impossible to buy or sell anything without the mark that identifies the beast. Contrary to popular belief, scripture does not support this doctrine. In Revelation 13:17, the phrase *buy or sell* isn't translated as a *phrase*. Its translation shows it as two individual words. The word, *buy,* means to purchase, and the word *sell* means to exchange for profit. Compare the same phrase *buy and sell* in James 4:13, and it is expressed or translated as a phrase or expression, which means to engage in business for profit as a merchant or tradesman. Putting it all in perspective, Revelation 13:17 is stating that no one could become a merchant in the Antichrist's kingdom unless that individual accepts the Mark of the Beast. Refusing the Mark of the Beast will not prevent anyone from going to the neighborhood store to buy a loaf of bread, but that individual could not be in the business of buying and selling merchandise on a corporate level.

Rev. 18:3   For all nations have drunk of the wine of the wrath of her fornication, and the kings of the earth have committed fornication with her, and

the merchants of the earth are waxed rich
through the abundance of her delicacies.

Rev. 18:11   And the merchants of the earth shall weep and
mourn over her; for no man buyeth their
merchandise any more:

Rev. 18:15   The merchants of these things, which were made
rich by her, shall stand afar off for the fear of her
torment, weeping and wailing,

Rev. 18: 23   And the light of a candle shall shine no more at
all in thee; and the voice of the bridegroom and
of the bride shall be heard no more at all in thee:
for thy merchants were the great men of the
earth; for by thy sorceries were all nations
deceived.

Revelation chapter 18 is further confirmation that the phrase
buy and sell is referencing conglomerate commerce. It is not
referencing individual consumers shopping for groceries. Babylon
is the Antichrist's kingdom, and the entire chapter describes the
fall of his empire. Four times the text references people who are
weeping and mourning due to the collapse of the Antichrist's
kingdom. Notice that it is only *merchants* that are grieving. It is the
merchants and not the individuals that accept the Mark of the
Beast with the expressed interest of climbing the corporate ladder.
The fall of Babylon will cause the net worth of the merchants to
tumble. The buying and selling mentioned in Revelation 13:16-17
isn't referencing buying groceries. This type of buying and selling
is only applicable at the corporate level.

A popular belief is that everyone that does not take the Mark
of the Beast would suffer execution. Scripture does not support
that theory. Antichrist will execute many people, but it's not for
refusing to accept the mark. Antichrist extinguishes anyone that
pose a threat to his plan. The consequence for refusing to accept
the Mark of the Beast is being denied the privilege of advancing or
prospering in Antichrist's kingdom.

Revelation, chapter 13, speaks of an Image that will stand in Jerusalem. It will also have the authority to pronounce judgment upon specific individuals. Any person that accepts the Mark of the Beast and refuses to worship the Image will face the executioner. Refusing to worship this Image is a direct insult and an open rejection of Antichrist himself.

It's not the Image that is enforcing the acceptance of the Mark of the Beast. The Image is only a personification of Antichrist. It is the False Prophet who empowers the Image. The False Prophet plans to ensure that everyone who receives the Mark of the Beast remains faithful to Antichrist. He controls the Image, with the allusion that the Image has a mind of its own. In reality, the Image is comparable to a puppet. The False Prophet commands it with the expressed purpose of enforcing loyalty to Antichrist.

Antichrist likes to imitate God. Just a God sealed the 144,000 to grant them protection; Antichrist will also put his mark on his elite group. Antichrist's mark identifies his loyal followers and guarantees their prosperity and welfare throughout his kingdom. The Mark of the Beast is applied directly to the bodies of anyone that endorses Antichrist as their God. The list of individuals that receives the Mark of the Beast is distinguished. It includes kings, chief executive officers, political and religious leaders.

People receive the Mark of the Beast's inscription in one of two places on the body; the forehead or the right hand. Scripture doesn't indicate why the location of the identifying mark can be on two different areas on the body. Perhaps the site of the *mark* means the rank or security clearance of each person that receives it.

Scripture does not indicate whether or not the mark will be visible to the naked eye. It's conceivable to think that the mark will be visible, so Antichrist's constituents will be readily identifiable. With the advancement in technology, perhaps smart-scanners will be stationed at strategic checkpoints to verify who's who. It's also possible that the mark glows when the individual passes by an area designated as a hot zone. For security purposes, the activation of lasers read all barcodes that enter the site. These barcodes can include credit cards, passports, driver licenses, bank accounts, or any documents that interest the Antichrist's regime.

Identifying the Mark of the Beast

It's common knowledge that Satan is cunning and deceptive. The Antichrist is a man that is influenced by Satan. That being the case, it stands to reason that Antichrist will adopt a few of Satan's deceptive practices. Most people are familiar with the number 666 and the consequences of accepting it. Because people are acquainted with the number 666, it would be difficult for anyone to receive any markings voluntarily on their person bearing the number 666. One deceptive tactic that he could use is the number system. The language of the New Testament is Greek. The nation of Israel speaks Hebrew, and the Roman government influenced that part of the world during Christ's ministry. Most people would immediately recognize 666, but what if Antichrist presents the number in Greek, Hebrew, or Italian? What if the authors spelled out the numbers rather than using binary numbers? For example, *six hundred sixty-six* is synonymous with 666, but the appearance is far different. Now take this approach a step further; suppose the application of these numbers is in Greek, Hebrew, or Italian. Would it be readily and easily identifiable as the Mark of the Beast?

Remember, the Mark of the Beast can be a number, a name, or a mark. Suppose Antichrist uses his name rather than the number. Suppose Antichrist uses his mark rather than the number. This subtle approach could be a beneficial tactic. Scripture does not give the mark's actual inscription, so how would one be sure that it is, or is not, the Mark of the Beast?

> Rev. 16:2 And the first went, and poured out his vial upon the earth; and there fell a noisome and grievous sore upon the men which had the Mark of the Beast, and *upon* them which worshipped his image.

When God begins to pour out His Wrath, the body of every individual that received the Mark of the Beast will immediately become diseased. In an instant, an atrocious sore will manifest itself on parts of their anatomy. Perhaps that sore will form on the very spot where they received the Mark of the Beast. The formation of visible sores filled with puss on one's person indicates that Antichrist is an imposter. A person will receive this open sore because they accepted the Mark of the Beast, which is a disgusting abomination to the Lord. God distributes His first vial of Wrath by dispensing it upon all those individuals that received the Mark of the Beast. Warning. Do not accept any form of a name, a number, or a mark, on your body. Almighty God does not require anyone to take an inscription on their forehead or their hand. His identification is invisible because it is the spiritual circumcision of the heart (Rom. 2:29).

The Mark of the Beast is not limited to the number 666. A man should not be afraid of that number appearing in any form of identification, such as a social security number, driver's license number, or other identification documents. If you are engaged in any type of business transaction and the money to be refunded to you is in any form of 666, please accept the money because it is only a mathematical calculation. If the number 666 correlates with anything that requires denouncing God the Father, God the Son, or God the Holy Ghost, one should avoid it as though it is a plague (pun intended).

The Mark of the Beast can also be a name. Do not allow anyone to place any inscriptions or chips on your person if it has any association with God. There is only one God, and His name is Jehovah. Psalms 83:18 states, "That men may know that thou, whose name alone is JEHOVAH, art the most high over all the earth." He does not require a person to call Him by His name or receive any openly visible marks or inscriptions on their bodies. Circumcision is visible, but it was something that is private and not displayed publicly. His only requirement is that man must be born again. John 3:3 states, "...Verily, verily, I say unto thee, except a man be born again, he cannot see the kingdom of God." Do not accept or allow the inscription of the name of any God on your physical body. There only one exception concerning receiving a seal or mark on your forehead. God's seal is when angelic beings supernaturally seal one hundred and forty-four thousand individuals of Hebrew descent. Revelation 7:3-4 states, "Saying, Hurt not the earth, neither the sea, nor the trees, till we have sealed the servants of our God in their foreheads ... I heard the number of them which were sealed: and there were sealed an hundred and forty and four thousand of all the tribes of the children of Israel." The sealing of the 144,000 is a spiritual seal; not a physical seal.

CHAPTER 6

THE ABOMINATION OF DESOLATION

> Mat. 24:15 When ye therefore shall see the abomination of desolation, spoken of by Daniel the prophet, stand in the holy place, (whoso readeth, let him understand:)
>
> Mat. 24:16 Then let them which be in Judaea flee into the mountains:

THE setting of the above verses is in Jerusalem, Israel. The timing of this conversation is a few days before the crucifixion of Jesus. The disciples were asking Jesus about the End-times. Jesus was prophesying to the disciples concerning events taking place before the end of the world. He told them that when the Abomination of Desolation stands in the Holy Place, it would be very advantageous for Judea's inhabitants to flee into the mountains. The purpose of running from Judea is because there would be some troublesome times ahead. It would be the beginning of the Great Tribulation.

A Time of Trouble

> Mat. 24:21 For then shall be great tribulation, such as was not since the beginning of the world to this time, no, nor ever shall be.

Jesus continues to warn the disciples. He explains why people should flee into the mountains when they see the Abomination of Desolation. The Abomination of Desolation marks the beginning of a period consisting of extreme pressure and anguish. This devastating time is the Great Tribulation. It is a time of trouble that will be worse than any previous time on earth, and its severity can never occur again. When the people encounter the Abomination of Desolation standing in the Holy Place, immediately, they should recall Jesus' warning concerning this event. The instant the Abomination of Desolation is displayed, they should not hesitate even for a moment. They should flee immediately without taking the time to gather any of their belongings.

Mat. 24:15   When ye therefore shall see the abomination of desolation, spoken of by Daniel the prophet, stand in the holy place, (whoso readeth, let him understand:)

Mar. 13:14   But when ye shall see the abomination of desolation, spoken of by Daniel the prophet, standing where it ought not, (let him that readeth understand,) then let them that be in Judaea flee to the mountains:

Dan. 8:13   Then I heard one saint speaking, and another saint said unto that certain saint which spake, How long shall be the vision concerning the daily sacrifice, and the transgression of desolation, to give both the sanctuary and the host to be trodden under foot?

Dan. 9:27   And he shall confirm the covenant with many for one week: and in the midst of the week he shall cause the sacrifice and the oblation to cease, and for the overspreading of abominations he shall make it desolate, even until the consummation, and that determined shall be poured upon the desolate.

Dan. 11:31   And arms shall stand on his part, and they shall pollute the sanctuary of strength, and shall take away the daily sacrifice, and they shall place the abomination that maketh desolate.

Dan. 12:11 And from the time that the daily sacrifice shall be
taken away, and the abomination that maketh
desolate set up, there shall be a thousand two
hundred and ninety days.

Throughout scripture, only two men mention the
Abomination of Desolation. Jesus referenced it two different
times. The first time He mentioned it is in Matthew 24:15, and the
second time He mentioned it is in Mark 13:14. Each time Jesus
referenced the phrase *Abomination of Desolation,* the prophet Daniel
is cited as the source. Daniel spoke of it four different times, but
he never coined the idiom Abomination of Desolation. He
referenced it as an *abomination that makes one desolate.*

Pay close attention to all of Daniel's references to the
Abomination of Desolation. All four scripture verses have a
reference to a sacrifice, but three of them take it a step further and
label it as a *daily sacrifice.* That being the case, the Abomination of
Desolation is closely associated with how the Jewish people
worship. Somehow, traditional Jewish worship will no longer be
acceptable because it will be replaced by worshipping something
other than Almighty God. The Hebrew people are encouraged to
worship a different entity as their God.

Exo. 20:3 Thou shalt have no other gods before me.
Exo. 20:4 Thou shalt not make unto thee any graven image,
or any likeness of any thing that is in heaven
above, or that is in the earth beneath, or that is in
the water under the earth:

Deu. 27:15 Cursed be the man that maketh any graven or
molten image, an abomination unto the LORD,
the work of the hands of the craftsman, and
putteth it in a secret place. And all the people shall
answer and say, Amen.

In the Ten Commandments, God explicitly stated that man is
not allowed to make any graven images or idols. He established
this law because He knew the people would bow down and

worship the images or idols instead of worshipping Him. Be assured; God does not share His glory with any other god. Anyone making a graven image or an idol is cursed because God deems it to be an abomination.

Deu. 7:25   The graven images of their gods shall ye burn with fire: thou shalt not desire the silver or gold that is on them, nor take it unto thee, lest thou be snared therein: for it is an abomination to the LORD thy God.

Deu. 7:26   Neither shalt thou bring an abomination into thine house, lest thou be a cursed thing like it: but thou shalt utterly detest it, and thou shalt utterly abhor it; for it is a cursed thing.

Any graven images that man worships, as God is an abomination. A man should not even desire the gold or the silver used to create those idols or images. God does not want anyone to worship anything that humanity himself has made, but God wants man to worship his Creator.

It's incredibly problematic that man will create his own God, but to bring a human-made god into one's house and worship it, will be utterly detested by God. Now imagine the repercussions if someone takes a human-made idol into God's place of worship. Creating a graven image is an abomination, but worshipping a created graven image is what brings about *desolation*. The Abomination of Desolation is worshipping a human-made graven image or idol as Almighty God.

Rev. 13:10   He that leadeth into captivity shall go into captivity: he that killeth with the sword must be killed with the sword. Here is the patience and the faith of the saints.

Rev. 13:11   And I beheld another beast coming up out of the earth; and he had two horns like a lamb, and he spake as a dragon.

Rev. 13:12 And he exerciseth all the power of the first beast before him, and causeth the earth and them which dwell therein to worship the first beast, whose deadly wound was healed.

Rev. 13:13 And he doeth great wonders, so that he maketh fire come down from heaven on the earth in the sight of men,

Rev. 13:14 And deceiveth them that dwell on the earth by the means of those miracles which he had power to do in the sight of the beast; saying to them that dwell on the earth, that they should make an image to the beast, which had the wound by a sword, and did live.

Rev. 13:15 And he had power to give life unto the image of the beast, that the image of the beast should both speak, and cause that as many as would not worship the image of the beast should be killed.

The Holy Spirit is the animated force of the triune Godhead. It's responsible for convicting Christians when they miss the mark or commit sin, but it never requisitions anyone to sin. Just as the Holy Spirit is God, Satan will create an imposter (Image) representing the Antichrist as God. The Image is not a person, but it is a figure made in Antichrist's likeness, the person who proclaims to be God. It is an animated force. Perhaps it is a 3-D hologram that represents the Antichrist during his absence from the City of Jerusalem. Holograms can be seen and heard but not touched; therefore, one perceives it as a spirit. Because the Image is falsely accommodating the Holy Spirit's office, many individuals deceitfully worship it as the *Holy Spirit,* thus signifying Blasphemy of the Holy Ghost. The Image is in opposition to the Holy Spirit; therefore, this act constitutes blasphemy. It is the Image that is the Abomination of Desolation. The mere fact that it stands in the Holy Place as God establishes an even greater abomination. It demands the people to worship it as the Holy Spirit. The final destiny of anyone who worships the Image as the Holy Spirit is eternal damnation. The Image mentioned in Revelation, chapter 13, is the Abomination of Desolation of which Jesus spoke (Mat.

24:15). The Abomination of Desolation, mentioned by Daniel, is the Image made in the likeness of the Beast (Antichrist). The False Prophet ordered the construction of this Image so that the people could worship it as God (Rev. 13:14). The Image is the Abomination of Desolation because the intended purpose of it is to receive reverence as Almighty God.

CHAPTER 7

THE IMAGE

THE Abomination of Desolation is an Image. The appearance of it is in the likeness of the Antichrist. The Image imposes the penalty of death upon all of those individuals that refuse to worship it. The Image is responsible for pioneering the implementation of the Mark of the Beast. Listed below are some of the characteristics that describe the Abomination of Desolation.

- Who   not a person; its Antichrist personified
- What   it is an image or a hologram
- When   in the middle of the Tribulation Period
- Where it stands in the temple
- Why   so that humanity can worship it
- How   False Prophet ordered man to make it

We know the Image referenced in Revelation chapter 13 is the Abomination of Desolation. The introduction of this Image is during the middle of the Tribulation Period. From the beginning of time, man has faced and struggled with the idea of some form of tribulation. We know the struggles of the End-times holds the classification of the Great Tribulation. All grief and anguish is great or extreme when you are in the midst of it, but why is this trial that's being initiated by the Abomination of Desolation more severe than any other tribulation?

In the world today, we have people losing homes, jobs, religious freedoms, life savings, etc. Those people are experiencing severe tribulation, but those trials are not the Great Tribulation that corresponds directly with the Abomination of Desolation. How is the Tribulation imposed by the Image any different from the struggles many people face every day?

Rev. 13:1   And I stood upon the sand of the sea, and saw a beast rise up out of the sea, having seven heads and ten horns, and upon his horns ten crowns, and upon his heads the name of blasphemy.

The Beast Rising Out of the Sea

Revelation chapter 13 explains the Abomination of Desolation. It is associated with a few unsavory characters during the End-times that shape governmental indoctrination and restrict religious freedoms. The chapter begins with a beast rising out of the sea. Scripture identifies the beast rising out of the sea, as a kingdom. The leader of this kingdom is a man, commonly known to be the Antichrist. The dragon or Satan empowers the Antichrist and his empire; therefore, everything about this kingdom is iniquitous.

Rev. 13:5   And there was given unto him a mouth speaking great things and blasphemies; and power was given unto him to continue forty *and* two months.

Antichrist is an excellent speaker. When he speaks, it is quite powerful and convincing. Remember, Antichrist's power and authority come from Satan, so he is compelling, hypnotic, and deceptive. Satan portrays to be a roaring lion, with the expressed purpose of seeking whom he can destroy. Antichrist is no different. His only mission is to eradicate man by manipulating his religious beliefs to control who man worships as God.

Rev. 13:6   And he opened his mouth in blasphemy against God, to blaspheme his name, and his tabernacle, and them that dwell in heaven.

Rev. 13:7   And it was given unto him to make war with the saints, and to overcome them: and power was given him over all kindreds, and tongues, and nations.

Just as the Antichrist's name implies, he is totally against God. Antichrist blasphemes God by stating that he is the only God that man can trust. He blasphemes God's name, declaring that Israel's God is too powerless and too passive to qualify as the God of the universe. He blasphemes God's tabernacle, insinuating heaven is here on earth where Antichrist reigns. Antichrist blasphemes God's angels, indicating they are devils rather than angels. He executes a war with the saints by forcing them to abandon Almighty God and worship him as their god. As he blasphemes Almighty God and forces people to worship him, he's establishing himself to be the only god the people will ever need.

> Rev. 13:11   And I beheld another beast coming up out of the earth; and he had two horns like a lamb, and he spake as a dragon.
> Rev. 13:12   And he exerciseth all the power of the first beast before him, and causeth the earth and them which dwell therein to worship the first beast, whose deadly wound was healed.

The Beast Rising Out of the Earth

As chapter 13 continues, there is another beast that rises out of the earth. This beast also symbolizes a kingdom, but it's not a political kingdom like the first beast that rose from the sea. The beast rising out of the earth is a faith-based kingdom. This kingdom and its leaders receive their power from Satan, just as the first beast's power originated from Satan. This beast has a lamb's appearance, but everything he does is blasphemous because his authority comes from the dragon (Satan). He appears to be a lamb, but in reality, he is imitating Jesus Christ, the Lamb of God. He plans to convince people that he is the one and only Messiah. According to scripture, Jesus was a prophet, so it is fitting to call the leader of this faith-based kingdom, *the False Prophet*.

In Bible prophecy, the word *horns* represent kings or nations. In this case, the word *horns* are referencing nations. Please note, the word *nations* do not necessarily mean different countries. According to Biblical definition, the word *nations* is Strong's #1484, and it means a group of people with the same ideology. Because the beast is a religious leader possessing two horns, he will be representing two nations or two religions. The setting of the End-time events is in the Middle-East, and the dominant religions in that region are Judaism and Islam. Scripture does not identify these two religions, but it is a good possibility that Judaism and Islam are the two religions that the False Prophet desires to unite.

> Rev. 13:13 And he doeth great wonders, so that he maketh fire come down from heaven on the earth in the sight of men,
>
> Rev. 13:14 And deceiveth them that dwell on the earth by *the means of* those miracles which he had power to do in the sight of the beast; saying to them that dwell on the earth, that they should make an image to the beast, which had the wound by a sword, and did live.

The False Prophet or Beast that comes out of the earth will have the authority to demonstrate signs and wonders because Satan is his power and dominance source. His powers and abilities will be limited, though; he can only employ them when he is in visual sight of the Antichrist. Although the False Prophet had authority as the Antichrist, he will be powerless whenever the Antichrist is not in his direct line of sight. For this reason, he ordered his followers to erect a statute (Image) of the Antichrist. The Image is a replica of Antichrist; therefore, it could remain in the False Prophet's presence, even when the Antichrist was out of town. The Image is an exact likeness of Antichrist; therefore, it makes it possible for the False Prophet to be empowered at all times, so long as the Image is in close proximity.

> Rev. 13:15 And he had power to give life unto the image of the beast, that the image of the beast should both speak, and cause that as many as would not worship the image of the beast should be killed.

The Authority of the Image

Constructive reasoning shows that the Image of Antichrist is the *Abomination of Desolation*. It is the Image that will be standing in the Holy Place. Matthew 24:15 states, "When ye therefore shall see the Abomination of Desolation, spoken of by Daniel the prophet, stand in the holy place." This Image will more than likely be some type of 3-D hologram operating under the False Prophet's orders. The Image will become animated and speak the False Prophet's programmed commands.

The Image will be a powerful force because it will be acting as Antichrist. People will understand that the Image is not Antichrist, the man, but accepts it as a disembodied spirit of Antichrist that administers rewards and (or) sanctions at will. In actuality, the False Prophet deceives the human race into believing that Antichrist and his Image, is Almighty God. The False Prophet has pioneered this illusion, that the Image's instructions, is God's will. He altered the narrative and persuaded the people to believe the following:

- It is the Image that causes humanity to take the mark
- It is the Image that sentences men to death
- It is the Image that allowing buying and selling

It isn't the Antichrist that is standing in the Holy Place impersonating God. It is the Image parading at the sacred place, declaring that he is the one and only God. Antichrist has already announced himself to be God; therefore, when the Image impersonates him, it is deemed to be Antichrist's spirit. It deceives many people into believing Antichrist is God; therefore, they accept the Image to be the spirit of God; in this case, it is the Spirit of Antichrist. The Image is referenced as the Abomination of Desolation because it proclaims to be the spirit of a false god, which is an abomination. Worshipping the Image as the spirit of a false god (Antichrist) is Blasphemy of the Holy Spirit. Blasphemy of the Holy Spirit is the only sin that renders permanent un-forgiveness; therefore, the Image standing in the temple of God proclaiming to be God is the Abomination of Desolation.

Satan is an imitator; there's nothing original about him. He doesn't create anything. He merely takes what God created and duplicates it with a slight twist, just enough of an alteration, to call it his own. Everything that God created is good, and everything that God said is the truth. Anything that God makes, and is used contrary to its intended purpose, is a perversion. Anytime you tweak the truth, it is no longer truth but a lie and originates from Satan.

Satan's Imitations

Rev. 7:3   Saying, Hurt not the earth, neither the sea, nor the trees, till we have sealed the servants of our God in their foreheads.

Rev. 13:16   And he causeth all, both small and great, rich and poor, free and bond, to receive a mark in their right hand, or in their foreheads:

God will seal His followers with an invisible seal on their forehead. Satan will force his followers to receive a visible mark either on his or her hand or forehead. Again, Satan is an imitator and not a creator. The only original thought or idea that Satan has ever initiated is iniquity.

Joh. 4:24   God *is* a Spirit: and they that worship him must worship *him* in spirit and in truth.

Rev. 13:14   And deceiveth them that dwell on the earth by *the means of* those miracles which he had power to do in the sight of the beast; saying to them that dwell on the earth, that they should make an image to the beast, which had the wound by a sword, and did live.

Rev. 13:15   And he had power to give life unto the image of the beast, that the image of the beast should both speak, and cause that as many as would not worship the image of the beast should be killed.

God desires people to worship Him voluntarily in spirit and truth. Satan demands and deceives his followers into worshipping him by any means necessary. God operates in love, while Satan, on the other hand, operates in fear.

Joh. 3:16   For God so loved the world, that he gave his only begotten Son, that whosoever believeth in him should not perish, but have everlasting life.

Mat. 4:8   Again, the devil taketh him up into an exceeding high mountain, and sheweth him all the kingdoms of the world, and the glory of them;

Mat. 4:9   And saith unto him, All these things will I give thee, if thou wilt fall down and worship me.

God promises His followers everlasting life for worshipping Him. Satan promises his followers fame and fortune for worshipping him. Please note, Satan never informs his followers that their fame and fortune is short-lived and limited to his or her life on earth.

God is invisible, and He is the creator of the universe, but Satan counters by producing a visible human being (Antichrist) with the intent to rule on earth. God loved the world so much that He sent us His Son as a prophet, but Satan counters by sending his followers a nameless False Prophet, perhaps even the biological son of Antichrist. God gave us the Holy Spirit to comfort us after the death, burial, resurrection, and ascension of His Son Jesus Christ the prophet. He sent the Holy Spirit to dwell within us and remind us of His teachings. Satan counters by creating an Image of a false god (Antichrist) to represent him. The Image is controlled by his False Prophet to give the illusions that Antichrist is multiple places as the same time. Please note, Jesus Christ is the only savior that has ever died for His followers, and also resurrected.

What comes to mind when you hear the phrase, God the Father, God the Son, and God the Holy Spirit? Most people think of the *HOLY TRINITY* or one God officiating in three different offices. On the other hand, Satan uses Antichrist to impersonate

God. He uses the False Prophet to mimic the Lamb of God. He uses the Image to imitate the spirit of God. These alterations by Satan reflect another TRINITY. The difference between the two trinities is God the Father, God the Son, and God the Holy Spirit is the *HOLY TRINITY*. At the same time, the Antichrist, the False Prophet, and the Image is an imitation or an *UNHOLY TRINITY*.

Mat. 12:31   Wherefore I say unto you, All manner of sin and blasphemy shall be forgiven unto men: but the blasphemy *against* the *Holy* Ghost shall not be forgiven unto men.

Mat .12:32   And whosoever speaketh a word against the Son of man, it shall be forgiven him: but whosoever speaketh against the Holy Ghost, it shall not be forgiven him, neither in this world, neither in the *world* to come.

Man possesses the possibility of forgiveness for all of his sins through repentance. This efficacy has one limitation. Man cannot receive forgiveness for Blasphemy of the Holy Spirit. Blasphemy is proclaiming something to be the opposite of its true nature or character. Worshipping the Image as the Holy Spirit is equivalent to saying the False Prophet is Jesus Christ and the Antichrist is God. Worshipping the Image of Antichrist is tantamount to Blasphemy of the Holy Spirit.

Rev. 14:9   And the third angel followed them, saying with a loud voice, If any man worship the beast and his image, and receive *his* mark in his forehead, or in his hand,

Rev. 14:10   The same shall drink of the wine of the wrath of God, which is poured out without mixture into the cup of his indignation; and he shall be tormented with fire and brimstone in the presence of the holy angels, and in the presence of the Lamb:

Rev. 14:11   And the smoke of their torment ascendeth up for
ever and ever: and they have no rest day nor
night, who worship the beast and his image, and
whosoever receiveth the mark of his name.

Remember, the Image is the Abomination of Desolation.
Anyone that worships the Image forfeits his or her salvation
forever. Just as the dove represents the Holy Spirit, the Image
represents the unholy spirit. If humanity believes the Image is holy,
then the corresponding response is to believe the dove does not
represent holiness, but something profane. This thought process is
blasphemy. Whosoever worships the Image as the Holy Spirit is
committing the Unpardonable Sin, which is Blasphemy of the Holy
Spirit. Worshipping the Image is the Abomination of Desolation,
simply because it is an abomination that leads to eternal
destruction.

Heb. 6:4   For *it is* impossible for those who were once
enlightened, and have tasted of the heavenly gift,
and were made partakers of the Holy Ghost,

Heb. 6:5   And have tasted the good word of God, and the
powers of the world to come,

Heb. 6:6   If they shall fall away, to renew them again unto
repentance; seeing they crucify to themselves the
Son of God afresh, and put *him* to an open shame.

Accepting the Mark of the Beast, worshipping the Beast, or
worshipping the image of the Beast, isn't the only way to commit
the Unpardonable Sin. There are other ways to achieve Blasphemy
of the Holy Spirit. There are several gifts of the Spirit listed in 1
Corinthians chapter 14, such as the gift of healing, the gift of
prophecy, the gift of miracles, etc. Every individual having these
gifts operating in their life is indeed acting by the Holy Spirit's
power. If that individual discovers another God and turns to
follow him in the future, that individual has just denounced or
blasphemed the Holy Spirit. Scripture clearly states that once a
person operates in the gifts of the Holy Spirit but later attributes
that heavenly gift to the power of another god, it is impossible to
repent of that transgression. Turning your back on the gifts of the

Holy Spirit is Blasphemy of the Holy Spirit because the Holy Spirit was once prevalent in that individual's life, and he or she later rejected it for a different god.

Can an individual accidentally blaspheme the Holy Spirit? The answer is NO. One must first know God and experience the gifts of the Holy Spirit before he is even eligible to commit such an atrocious sin. Once an individual knows the truth of God and has the gifts of the Holy Spirit operating in his or her life and then deliberately turn away and follow another god, that individual has just Blasphemed the Holy Spirit.

Is this to say that all backsliders are in danger of Blasphemy of the Holy Spirit? The answer to this question is NO. It's possible to be born-again and backslide, but that does not automatically qualify as the Unpardonable Sin. Yes, this action will affect that individual's salvation, but he can always repent and receive restoration as a born-again believer. On the other hand, if that same person was prominently operating in the gifts of the Holy Spirit, then suddenly abandoned his or her beliefs for another god, that individual is blaspheming the Holy Spirit and can never experience forgiveness for that transgression.

In the Bible, the number seven (7) is the number of completion, and the number six (6) is the number for man. The first person of the UNHOLY TRINITY is Antichrist, and he claims to be God. In reality, Antichrist is a man; therefore, the Antichrist's number is six. The second person of the UNHOLY TRINITY is the False Prophet, and he also claims to be God. In reality, the False Prophet is a man; therefore, the False Prophet's number is six. The third person of the UNHOLY TRINITY is the Image, and it represents the spirit of Antichrist. In reality, the Image represents a man; therefore, the Image's number is six. Respectively, combining the three biblical numbers for the three false Gods, the result is 666, which is recognized to be the Mark of the Beast.

There's a lot of emphasis placed on the number 666. Just what is the significance of this number? When trying to comprehend the meaning of this highly acknowledged number, consider that the number 666 is associated with something that's anti-god. Man attempts to represent God from three different aspects.

Jesus warned the disciples that when the Abomination of Desolation (Image) appears in the Holy Place, Judea's citizens should flee to the mountains. He wanted His people to be aware of the severity of the Image and its implications because it ushers in the Great Tribulation, which is the brainchild of the Antichrist and False Prophet. The Image's implementation initiates severe pain and suffering on the Jewish people while also sealing the eternal fate of all who worships it. The Image erected by the False Prophet is the Abomination of Desolation.

CHAPTER 8

THE SHEEP AND THE GOATS

Mat. 24:29 Immediately after the tribulation of those days shall the sun be darkened, and the moon shall not give her light, and the stars shall fall from heaven, and the powers of the heavens shall be shaken:

Mat. 24:30 And then shall appear the sign of the Son of man in heaven: and then shall all the tribes of the earth mourn, and they shall see the Son of man coming in the clouds of heaven with power and great glory.

Mat. 24:31 And he shall send his angels with a great sound of a trumpet, and they shall gather together his elect from the four winds, from one end of heaven to the other.

One Taken and the Other Left

WHEN Christ returns in the clouds; He will send His angels to gather together His saints. His return is an event that has several different designations. Based on doctrinal beliefs, His return is known as the Rapture, Second Coming, or First Resurrection. In this chapter, to minimize confusion, *His return* is referenced as *the First Resurrection*.

Matthew 24:29-31 brings us right up to the point of the First Resurrection. Matthew 24:32-39 is the beginning of two parables where Jesus is equating the blooming of a fig tree before harvest time to the events leading up to His return. He's comparing the world's unrighteousness in the days just before His return to the wickedness in the days of Noah. Mat. 24:32-39 are important, but they must be isolated so that the thought continues to flow directly from Mat. 24:31, to Mat. 24:40. By isolating Mat. 24:32-39, the text continues with Matthew 24:40-41, which gives a better understanding of His saints' gathering together.

Mat. 24:40   Then shall two be in the field; the one shall be taken, and the other left.

Mat. 24:41   Two *women shall be* grinding at the mill; the one shall be taken, and the other left.

At the First Resurrection, there will be the sound of a trumpet. Then, God dispatches the angels from heaven, with the expressed purpose of gathering together all the saints. The angels will be instructed to gather together only the elect. We know that everybody on earth will not be worthy enough to experience resurrection. When the angels come to harvest the world, they will take one (righteous), and the other (unrighteous) is left. The godly people are the ones that will meet the Lord in the air and will receive their spiritual bodies; their classification is the saints. Those individuals that are not deemed worthy enough to become a saint are left behind. Now we have two groups, the *ones-taken;* that is now in the presence of Christ and the *ones-left-behind;* that's still here on earth.

Jesus' Reigning on the Throne

As we continue to read Matthew chapter 24, we see more warnings and parables. Matthew 24:42-44 gives notice concerning being ready for His return because humanity does not know the hour of His return. Matthew 24:45-51 is a parable about the wise and unwise servants. Often when reading the Bible, a thought may not end with the completion of a chapter. Sometimes that same thought continues into the next chapter. That's what's happening in chapters 24 and 25. Chapter 25 is merely a continuation of Jesus giving parables concerning the End-times. Matthew 25:1-13 is a parable about ten virgins that's waiting for the bridegroom's return. Matthew 25:14-30 is another parable concerning how a man's servants conduct themselves while he is away traveling into a far country. All of these parables are referencing what man should be doing while awaiting Christ's return. Again, these verses are important, but if they are isolated so that the text can continue, one can better understand the precepts of the saints gathering together. The order in which one should read these verses, as though they are continuous, is Mat. 24:29-31, Mat. 24:40-41 and Mat. 25:32-46.

Mat. 25:31   When the Son of man shall come in his glory, and all the holy angels with him, then shall he sit upon the throne of his glory:

Mat. 25:32   And before him shall be gathered all nations: and he shall separate them one from another, as a shepherd divideth *his* sheep from the goats:

Immediately after the angels gather together the saints, Jesus will then begin to reign in His kingdom. Revelation 11:15 states, "The seventh angel sounded; and there were great voices in heaven, saying, the kingdoms of this world are become the kingdoms of our Lord, and of his Christ; and he shall reign for ever and ever." One of the first executive duties that Jesus will initiate when He begins to reign in His kingdom is to sit in judgment of the nations (ones left behind). He will divide these people as a shepherd separates his sheep from his goats.

The first thing we have to do is to determine the identity of the nations. We know that at the return of Jesus when He sends the angels to reap the earth, they segregate the people into two groups, the *ones-taken,* and the *ones-left-behind.* We know the saints are the ones chosen to be in the presence of Christ. Because they are in God's presence, they have already been judged. They were deemed to be righteous, because they are clothed their spiritual bodies. That leaves only the *ones-left-behind,* and Jesus must also sit in judgment to determine their fate. Those individuals that are *left behind* are the nations. It is the nations (people) that He separates into the sheep and the goats.

Remember, the nations are *left behind,* and now they too will have to be judged. The *nations* are the people that were not born-again at the moment that Christ returns. Confirmation that they aren't born-again is because they remain here on earth. Many believe the sheep nations are the saints and the goat nations are the sinners? Please note that the lines drawn on a map to designate a county's boundaries cannot determine whether a nation of people is righteous or unrighteous. There are moral and wicked people in every country; therefore, the separation of the sheep and goats does not establish countries' boundaries.

Scripture states that Jesus will separate the nations that are *left-behind* into two groups, namely the sheep and goats. If they are left behind because they are sinners, why are they further divided into two groups? There is something here concerning the nations that require a more in-depth examination.

The word *nations* do not necessarily mean it is a *country*. It can also mean a group of people with the same or similar beliefs and common goals. Some examples would be Judaism, Christianity, Islam, Buddhism, Democrats, Republicans, MADD, etc. Armed with this information concerning nations' definition, we can see that the nations (people) had one common denominator. None of them followed the laws of God; therefore, none of them were born-again. Now Jesus will further divide the nations (people) based on some of their other common differences.

Jesus will divide the nations into two groups, known as the sheep and the goats. The sheep are what we call generic Christians. An example of sheep is an individual that possesses an arsenal of good moral values and they are law-abiding citizens but are not born-again. The goats, on the other hand, are individuals that have almost no moral values at all. They openly rebelled against neighbors, local authorities, governments, Almighty God, etc. The goats are people that possess a reprobate mind and are guilty of blaspheming the Holy Ghost. Matthew 12:32 states, "Whosoever speaketh against the Holy Ghost, it shall not be forgiven him, neither in this world, neither in the world to come."

Rewarding the Sheep

Mat. 25:33   And he shall set the sheep on his right hand, but the goats on the left.

Mat. 25:34   Then shall the King say unto them on his right hand, Come, ye blessed of my Father, inherit the kingdom prepared for you from the foundation of the world:

When Jesus separates the sheep from the goats, He will place the sheep on His right side and the goats on His left side. He will then invite the sheep to inherit the kingdom whose preparation was from earth's creation. Many understand this verse to mean that Jesus is asking the sheep to inherit the kingdom of Heaven to dwell with Him forever. No, the saints were the *ones-taken, and* they have already taken up residency in the kingdom of Heaven. They are already in the presence of God, with their new spiritual bodies. The sheep are a part of the nations or the *ones-left-behind*. The kingdom that the sheep are inheriting is the earthly Millennial kingdom, where the saints will rule and reign over them. They do not have spiritual or glorified bodies like the saints (Body of Christ). The sheep are the law-abiding people who never surmised that God was genuine, so they never accepted Christ as their Lord and Savior. They will reside in the Millennial kingdom, which is here on earth. Matthew 5:5 states, "Blessed are the meek: for they shall inherit the earth." The saints will rule over the sheep right here on earth. Revelation 1:6 states, "And hast made us unto our God kings and priests: and we shall reign on the earth."

Mat. 24:35   For I was an hungred, and ye gave me meat: I was thirsty, and ye gave me drink: I was a stranger, and ye took me in:

Mat. 25:36   Naked, and ye clothed me: I was sick, and ye visited me: I was in prison, and ye came unto me.

Mat. 25:37   Then shall the righteous answer him, saying, Lord, when saw we thee an hungred, and fed *thee?* or thirsty, and gave *thee* drink?

Mat. 25:38   When saw we thee a stranger, and took *thee* in? or naked, and clothed *thee?*

Mat. 25:39   Or when saw we thee sick, or in prison, and came unto thee?

Mat. 25:40   And the King shall answer and say unto them, Verily I say unto you, Inasmuch as ye have done *it* unto one of the least of these my brethren, ye have done *it* unto me.

Jesus explained to the sheep the reason He chose them to enter the Millennial kingdom. He grants the sheep a second chance because they were law-abiding citizens and expressed love and compassion to others during their lifetime. That love they conveyed to others was a reflection of their love for Jesus. The sheep realize that they are unworthy but failed to understand why Jesus stated that they showered Him with love. They asked Jesus, when was He in trouble, and when did they convey any love to him? Jesus explains to them that as much as they extended love to their fellow man, they were expressing their love toward him. Matthew 22:37-39 indicates that man should first love God with all of his heart, and second, he should love his neighbor as himself. Although the sheep did not repent, they did show love to their neighbors, which was a direct reflection of the love they possessed in their hearts. By showing love to their neighbors, they were expressing their affection for God, but without repenting.

Rewarding the Goats

Mat. 25:41   Then shall he say also unto them on the left hand, Depart from me, ye cursed, into everlasting fire, prepared for the devil and his angels:

After rewarding the sheep, Jesus will then turn His attention to the goats. He will determine that the goats lived a vile lifestyle, and He will then pass judgment upon them and sentence them to Hell forever. Initially, The Lord did not design Hell for human beings because He created Adam to live forever. Because of the disobedience of the fallen angels, God created *Hell* (2Pe. 2:4). Hell is a tormenting compartment, and it has a standing reservation for the Devil and his angels. Because the goats had a reprobate mind and refused to repent, they aligned themselves with the Devil; therefore, the Lord sentences them to Hell-fire.

Mat. 25:42   For I was an hungred, and ye gave me no meat: I was thirsty, and ye gave me no drink:
Mat. 25:43   I was a stranger, and ye took me not in: naked, and ye clothed me not: sick, and in prison, and ye visited me not.

Mat. 25:44   Then shall they also answer him, saying, Lord, when saw we thee an hungred, or athirst, or a stranger, or naked, or sick, or in prison, and did not minister unto thee?

Mat. 25:45   Then shall he answer them, saying, Verily I say unto you, Inasmuch as ye did *it* not to one of the least of these, ye did *it* not to me.

Jesus explains to the goats, the reason they are not allowed to reside in the Millennial kingdom and why He's sentencing them to spend eternity in Hell-fire. The goats receive eternal damnation because they lived solely to saturate their lives with selfishness and fleshly lusts. They only expressed their love to themselves and to others that had a similar mindset. Because they failed to extend love and kindness to others, they were saying that they contained no love for God. 1 John 4:7 states, "Let us love one another: for love is of God; and every one that loveth is born of God, and knoweth God."

Mat. 25:46   And these shall go away into everlasting punishment: but the righteous into life eternal.

The people *left behind* are the nations, and they will undergo further separation into two distinct groups, called the sheep and the goats. Remember, both groups are *left-behind;* therefore, they will be classified as unworthy to be called saints at Christ's return. The sheep will reside in the Millennial kingdom while the goats dwell in eternal Hell-fire. The sheep are the people that will populate the earth after the return of Christ. The sheep will be under the authority of the resurrected saints. Revelation 2:26 states, "He that overcometh, and keepeth my works unto the end, to him will I give power over the nations."

The goats shall go into everlasting punishment while the sheep inherit the physical Millennial kingdom. The sheep aren't the resurrected saints. The sheep remain behind only because they failed to repent. The saints are the *ones-taken.* The angels took them because they were genuinely born-again, and their lifestyle deemed them worthy of eternal life. The resurrected saints will enter eternal life; the sheep will enter into the Millennial kingdom, and the goats will descend into eternal Hell-fire.

Chapter 9

THE BATTLE OF ARMAGEDDON

Rev. 16:16   And he gathered them together into a place called in the Hebrew tongue Armageddon.

ARMAGEDDON is only mentioned by name once, in the KJV of the Bible. Many believe it is the deadliest battle ever to take place on earth. There are many unanswered questions concerning the Battle of Armageddon. The following are a few of those unanswered questions.

- What is the Battle of Armageddon?
- Why is the Battle of Armageddon fought?
- Where is the Battle of Armageddon fought?
- When is the Battle of Armageddon fought?
- How long does the Battle of Armageddon last?
- Who fights in the Battle of Armageddon?

What is the Battle of Armageddon?

Rev. 11:15   And the seventh angel sounded; and there were great voices in heaven, saying, The kingdoms of this world are become *the kingdoms* of our Lord, and of his Christ; and he shall reign for ever and ever.

Rev. 11:16   And the four and twenty elders, which sat before God on their seats, fell upon their faces, and worshipped God,

Rev. 11:17   Saying, We give thee thanks, O Lord God Almighty, which art, and wast, and art to come; because thou hast taken to thee thy great power, and hast reigned.

Rev. 11:18 And the nations were angry, and thy wrath is come, and the time of the dead, that they should be judged, and that thou shouldest give reward unto thy servants the prophets, and to the saints, and them that fear thy name, small and great; and shouldest destroy them which destroy the earth.

The Battle of Armageddon is the last physical battle in this dispensation of time. It is when Christ returns to establish His everlasting kingdom right here on earth. It is the termination of man's domination of the kingdoms of this world. It is a time when all born-again saints, both alive and dead, will be rewarded for their faithfulness to the Word of God while all others will be subject to God's Wrath.

Why is the Battle of Armageddon Necessary?

Dan. 9:24 Seventy weeks are determined upon thy people and upon thy holy city, to finish the transgression, and to make an end of sins, and to make reconciliation for iniquity, and to bring in everlasting righteousness, and to seal up the vision and prophecy, and to anoint the most Holy.

The purpose of the Battle of Armageddon is so that God can terminate the transgressions of His covenant. The human race continued its involvement in sin, beginning with Adam's disobedience. The Battle of Armageddon finalizes the practice of sin, and at the same time, it re-establishes God's relationship with the saints. One of the main advantages of this great battle is to anoint Jesus Christ as Lord of Lords and King of Kings.

When Jesus died on the cross, He fulfilled the requirement of all blood sacrifices in the Old Testament. John 19:30 states, "It is finished: and he bowed his head, and gave up the ghost." Jesus' death parallels the fulfillment of Grace under the New

Testament. Revelation 16:17 states, "There came a great voice out of the temple of heaven, from the throne, saying, it is done." The Battle of Armageddon is the end of the Covenant of Grace and the beginning of a period where people can experience heaven on earth for the first time since Adam's expulsion from the Garden of Eden.

Where is the Battle of Armageddon Fought?

Many scholars submit that the battlefield for the Battle of Armageddon is in Israel, known as Megiddo or the Jezreel Valley. The actual location of this valley is northern Israel. This valley has been the battleground of numerous other battles simply because of its strategic location.

Rev. 16:12   And the sixth angel poured out his vial upon the great river Euphrates; and the water thereof was dried up, that the way of the kings of the east might be prepared.

Rev. 9:14   Saying to the sixth angel which had the trumpet, Loose the four angels which are bound in the great river Euphrates.

Rev. 9:15   And the four angels were loosed, which were prepared for an hour, and a day, and a month, and a year, for to slay the third part of men.

Rev. 9:16   And the number of the army of the horsemen *were* two hundred thousand thousand: and I heard the number of them.

Scripture mentions the Euphrates River drying up to provide an avenue for the kings from the east to assemble for the Battle of Armageddon. The Kings of the East will gather a great army that is 200,000,000 soldiers in strength. The military has orders to kill and they will succeed to massacre about one-third of all the people in the region of the Euphrates River. If the scholars are right in stating the Battle is fought in the Jezreel

Valley, then the battle is fought on multiple fronts because the Euphrates River does not run through Israel. It runs north of Israel, from Turkey through Syria to Iraq.

When is the Battle of Armageddon Fought?

The timing of the Battle of Armageddon is a very narrow window. The Euphrates River dries up when God pours out the sixth vial of His Wrath. The Wrath of God consists of a total of seven vials of punishment. He pours out the vials in succession. The association that Armageddon has with the Euphrates River, is that it dries up to prepare a thoroughfare for the military.

God begins to pour out His Wrath immediately after the return of Christ for His saints. God's Wrath cannot start until all of the saints are resurrected and gathered in the presence of the Lord. 1 Thessalonians 5:9 states, "God hath not appointed us to wrath, but to obtain salvation by our Lord Jesus Christ." When Christ returns for His saints, the Battle of Armageddon takes center stage. The timing of this great battle is after the resurrection of the saints but preceding the Millennium. After the Battle of Armageddon, there's only one more vial to be poured out. The outpouring of the seventh vial of Wrath marks the beginning of the Millennial age.

Time-span of the Battle of Armageddon

Throughout history, most wars last for years, sometimes even decades. Israel has engaged in lots of battles throughout the years, but her recent wars have not lasted years, but only a few days. Perhaps the Battle of Armageddon should receive the classification of a police action rather than a war. The main reason Christ will return to earth for His saints is to stamp out iniquity, once and for all. When He returns, it will not take Him an excessive amount of time to clean up unrighteousness. Zechariah 3:9 states, "I will remove the iniquity of that land in one day." Babylon also is *the mystery city* that's ruling over the kings of the earth during the End-times. The city of Babylon will fall in one day. Revelation 18:8 states, "Her plagues come in one day, death, and mourning, and famine; and she shall be utterly burned with fire: for strong is the Lord God who judgeth her." Yes, Babylon will fall in one day, but it will not take all day to accomplish its destruction. The total amount of allotted time for the destruction of Babylon is one hour. Revelation 18:10 states, "That great city Babylon, that mighty city! for in one hour is thy judgment come."

The capital of the final kingdom is Babylon. Initially, it was a confederacy of ten kings. Later, the ten kings align themselves with the Antichrist and relinquish their authority to him. They will rule with him for only one hour. Revelation 17:12 states, "But receive power as kings one hour with the beast."

The Battle of Armageddon will last for approximately one hour. Remember, this is a war, it is man versus God. It is not a fair contest by any stretch of the imagination. Man will be using conventional weaponry, including nuclear weapons, but God's weapon of choice is the Sword of the Spirit, the Word of God. He will merely speak defeat upon His enemies, and the battle will come to an abrupt end. Revelation 19:15 states, "And out of his mouth goeth a sharp sword, that with it he should smite the nations: and he shall rule them with a rod of iron: and he treadeth the winepress of the fierceness and wrath of Almighty God." The Battle of Armageddon will last about one hour, but the outpouring of all seven vials of the wrath of God reaches completion in one day.

Who Fights in the Battle of Armageddon?

Rev. 17:12   And the ten horns which thou sawest are ten kings, which have received no kingdom as yet; but receive power as kings one hour with the beast.

Rev. 17:13   These have one mind, and shall give their power and strength unto the beast.

Rev. 17:14   These shall make war with the Lamb, and the Lamb shall overcome them: for he is Lord of

lords, and King of kings: and they that are with
him *are* called, and chosen, and faithful.

The Battle of Armageddon is a battle that's fought between
the Lamb and a Beast. The Lamb is Jesus, and the Beast is the
Antichrist. The recently resurrected saints will join with Jesus,
and the Antichrist aligns with a ten-nation federation that
loathes the Nation of Israel. This battle is a battle of
righteousness versus unrighteousness. Many years ago, Enoch
prophesied about this great war. Jude 1:4-15 states, "...The
Lord cometh with ten thousands of his saints, to execute
judgment upon all, and to convince all that are ungodly among
them of all their ungodly deeds..." The Lord and the saints join
together against Antichrist and his followers in the Battle of
Armageddon. This war is designed to execute judgment upon
the wicked and usher in a world filled with peace.

The Battle of Armageddon Weapons of Choice

The weapon used by Jesus and the saints in the Battle of
Armageddon is a sword. Compared to modern-day weaponry,
this weapon seems to be a little primitive, but it is not just any
sword. This sword is a potent weapon because it is a double-
edged sword. Another defining point about this particular
sword is that it has a great sheath. Revelation. 1:16 states, "And
out of his mouth went a sharp twoedged sword."

Being armed with a sword with two edges in one's mouth
seems to be a little dangerous. The two-edged weapon is no
ordinary sword. It is a unique sword with extraordinary
characteristics. It is the Sword of the Spirit. Ephesians 6:17 states,
"And take the helmet of salvation, and the sword of the Spirit,
which is the word of God." The weapon of choice used by Jesus
and the saints is the Word of God. Jesus merely speaks His word
to defeat the enemy. Revelation. 19:15 states, "Out of his mouth
goeth a sharp sword, that with it he should smite the nations." The
characteristics of this sword also parallel with Isaiah's prophecy.

Isaiah 11:4 states, "And with the breath of his lips shall he slay the wicked."

> Eze. 38:4   And I will turn thee back, and put hooks into thy jaws, and I will bring thee forth, and all thine army, horses and horsemen, all of them clothed with all sorts *of armour, even* a great company *with* bucklers and shields, all of them handling swords:

According to the book of Ezekiel, the weapons of the Antichrist and his coalition's will consist of shields, bucklers, and swords. We must remember that Ezekiel spoke of his day's weapons, which are primitive compared to today's weapons. More than likely, Antichrist and his allies will be using conventional weapons of today, such as machine guns, tanks, bombs, airplanes, etc.

God will use the sword of His mouth by speaking His enemies' defeat into existence while Antichrist will be fighting with conventional weapons. Perhaps Antichrist's weapons will include small nuclear arms, but not powerful enough to destroy Israel. Joel 3:20 states, "Judah shall dwell for ever." Armed with the knowledge that Judah's destruction never comes into fruition, should comfort born-again believers that are concerned about Middle-eastern nations acquiring access to nuclear weapons. Even if Israel's enemies are victorious in developing or acquiring nuclear weapons, God will see to it that they malfunction if ever deployed against the Nation of Israel.

What Nation does Antichrist Represent?

We know that Antichrist will fight in the Battle of Armageddon, but what is his nation of descent? Many scholars have predicted that his country of origin will probably be Russia. Others say he will be Jewish, and still, others say he will be a Muslim. To better understand Antichrist's nation of origin, we need to go to the book of Ezekiel.

Eze. 38:1 And the word of the LORD came unto me, saying,

Eze. 38:2 Son of man, set thy face against Gog, the land of Magog, the chief prince of Meshech and Tubal, and prophesy against him,

Please note, just because an individual is born in a particular country, that doesn't necessarily mean that his leadership role reflects the ideology of his country of birth. He could be from any country, just as other organizations' leaders, such as ISIS, Al-Qaeda, PLO, etc. The first thing we have to do in determining Antichrist's origin is to understand Gog's meaning. Who or what is Gog? The word *Gog* appears in the KJV of the Bible in four separate chapters and three different forms. In 1 Chronicles chapter 5, it is a man's name. In Ezekiel chapters 38 and 39, it appears as a northern kingdom. In Revelation chapter 20, it seems to be a title.

Ezekiel 38:2 identifies Gog as a chief prince reigning over the land of Magog. Now we have to determine the identity of this chief prince. To understand what scripture means when it references *a chief prince,* we have to go to the book of Daniel.

Dan. 10:1 In the third year of Cyrus king of Persia a thing was revealed unto Daniel, whose name was called Belteshazzar; and the thing *was* true, but the time appointed *was* long: and he understood the thing, and had understanding of the vision.

Dan. 10:2 In those days I Daniel was mourning three full weeks.

Dan. 10:3 I ate no pleasant bread, neither came flesh nor wine in my mouth, neither did I anoint myself at all, till three whole weeks were fulfilled.

Daniel had a vision revealed to him from God. He understood the concept was going to be some time in the future, but he was having trouble understanding the vision's particulars.

He decided that he would pray and fast, asking God to clarify the vision's meaning. Daniel prayed for twenty-one days without receiving an answer.

After three weeks had passed, suddenly Daniel saw a man clothed in linen and the man began to speak to him. Daniel, being fearful, lost consciousness and collapsed on the ground.

Dan. 10:10 And, behold, an hand touched me, which set me upon my knees and *upon* the palms of my hands.

Dan. 10:11 And he said unto me, O Daniel, a man greatly beloved, understand the words that I speak unto thee, and stand upright: for unto thee am I now sent. And when he had spoken this word unto me, I stood trembling.

Dan. 10:12 Then said he unto me, Fear not, Daniel: for from the first day that thou didst set thine heart to understand, and to chasten thyself before thy God, thy words were heard, and I am come for thy words.

Dan. 10:13 But the prince of the kingdom of Persia withstood me one and twenty days: but, lo, Michael, one of the chief princes, came to help me; and I remained there with the kings of Persia.

We know the man that Daniel saw clothed in linen is Gabriel. Daniel 8:16 states, "Gabriel, make this man to understand the vision." Gabriel is an archangel; just as Michael is an archangel. Gabriel is a chief prince just as Michael is a chief prince; therefore, a chief prince is a high-ranking angelic being. Because the Prince of Persia is opposing an angel of God, it stands to reason, the Prince of Persia is a celestial being also.

The reference made to a prince in Ezekiel 38:1-2 isn't talking about a mortal man. It is referencing the chief prince (angelic being); therefore, Gog is the chief prince, and Gog is none other than Satan himself.

Scripture also pointed out that Gog was the chief prince of Meshech and Tubal. Every leader must have a territory or domain over which he reigns. The same applies to Gog. Just as the prince's realm that fought against Gabriel was Persia, Gog's kingdom is Meshech and Tubal.

Another word that deserves attention is the word *Magog*. The name *Magog* means *a northern region*. Magog or the northern region is the territory that is under the authority of Gog. Sometimes in scripture, the word *Magog* references Gog's inhabitants or followers. This reference is synonymous with the people of a nation or territory. Revelation 20:8 states, "And shall go out to deceive the nations which are in the four quarters of the earth, Gog and Magog, to gather them together to battle."

Identifying the Battle of Armageddon?

Some scholars have determined that Ezekiel 38 and 39 is not the Battle of Armageddon. They seem to think that Ezekiel 38 and 39 is a battle that will precede the Rapture. This viewpoint leads to the notion that there will be approximately seven more years before the beginning of the Battle of Armageddon. These seven years are called the Tribulation Period.

> Eze. 39:9   And they that dwell in the cities of Israel shall go forth, and shall set on fire and burn the weapons, both the shields and the bucklers, the bows and the arrows, and the handstaves, and the spears, and they shall burn them with fire seven years:

Many scholars use Ezekiel 39:9 to support the viewpoint of the Pre-Tribulation Rapture. They ascertain that this war is not the Battle of Armageddon, but it is a war that precedes the Tribulation Period. After this war and after the enemy's defeat, the Jewish survivors will collect the enemy's weapons left on the battlefield. They will burn those weapons for seven years, which coincides with the length of the Tribulation Period.

As stated before, many scholars believe Ezekiel 38 and 39 are referencing a war that precedes the Tribulation Period. Upon closer examination, scripture appears to support the fact that Ezekiel 38 and 39 is the Battle of Armageddon.

Eze. 38:18 And it shall come to pass at the same time when Gog shall come against the land of Israel, saith the Lord GOD, *that* my fury shall come up in my face.

Eze. 38:19 For in my jealousy *and* in the fire of my wrath have I spoken, Surely in that day there shall be a great shaking in the land of Israel;

Eze. 38:20 So that the fishes of the sea, and the fowls of the heaven, and the beasts of the field, and all creeping things that creep upon the earth, and all the men that *are* upon the face of the earth, shall shake at my presence, and the mountains shall be thrown down, and the steep places shall fall, and every wall shall fall to the ground.

Eze. 38:21 And I will call for a sword against him throughout all my mountains, saith the Lord GOD: every man's sword shall be against his brother.

Eze. 38:22 And I will plead against him with pestilence and with blood; and I will rain upon him, and upon his bands, and upon the many people that *are* with him, an overflowing rain, and great hailstones, fire, and brimstone.

Eze. 38:23 Thus will I magnify myself, and sanctify myself; and I will be known in the eyes of many nations, and they shall know that I *am* the LORD.

Rev. 16:18 And there were voices, and thunders, and lightnings; and there was a great earthquake, such as was not since men were upon the earth, so mighty an earthquake, *and* so great.

Rev. 16:19 And the great city was divided into three parts, and the cities of the nations fell: and great

Babylon came in remembrance before God, to give unto her the cup of the wine of the fierceness of his wrath.

Rev. 16:20 And every island fled away, and the mountains were not found.

Rev. 16:21 And there fell upon men a great hail out of heaven, *every stone* about the weight of a talent: and men blasphemed God because of the plague of the hail; for the plague thereof was exceeding great.

When Gog comes against Israel, God's fury will rise. The anger of God's Wrath will cause a shaking in the land. All life forms will shake in God's presence; even mountains cannot stand. There will be overflowing rain, hailstones, fire, and brimstone. God will magnify himself so that everyone knows His name throughout the earth. These events parallel with Revelation 16:18-20. There will be thunder, lightning, earthquakes, hail, and mountains and islands will no longer be in existence.

Eze. 39:7 So will I make my holy name known in the midst of my people Israel; and I will not *let them* pollute my holy name any more: and the heathen shall know that I *am* the LORD, the Holy One in Israel.

Eze. 39:8 Behold, it is come, and it is done, saith the Lord GOD; this *is* the day whereof I have spoken.

Rev. 16:17 And the seventh angel poured out his vial into the air; and there came a great voice out of the temple of heaven, from the throne, saying, It is done.

God said He would make His holy name known amid Israel. He will not let ungodly men pollute His holy name any longer. The heathen shall know that God Almighty is the Holy One of Israel. Ezekiel 39:7-8 and Revelation 16:17 shares an identical phrase; *it is done.* These passages signify the end of this present age and the beginning of the Millennial kingdom. Based on these scriptures, it is impossible to have another seven years where Antichrist will be running rampant?

God stated that after this battle, Israel would know Him forever. Ezekiel 39:22 states, "The house of Israel shall know that I am the LORD their God from that day and forward." When the battle is complete, God will no longer hide His presence from Israel. Ezekiel 39:29 states, "Neither will I hide my face any more from them: for I have poured out my spirit upon the house of Israel." The conclusion of this battle does not bring seven more years of Tribulation by Antichrist, but it initiates the end of this present age of Grace and ushers in the Millennial kingdom. Ezekiel 38 and 39 is not a war that precedes the Tribulation Period; it is the Battle of Armageddon, which concludes this present age of Grace.

What Nation Leads the Invasion?

Eze. 38:2   Son of man, set thy face against Gog, the land of Magog, the chief prince of Meshech and Tubal, and prophesy against him,

Scholars say that Russia is Meshech and Tubal, and Russia will be leading the coalition that invades Israel in the last days. Ezekiel 38:2 mentions several nations, but Russia isn't one of them. It's ironic how it's concluded that Russia leads this coalition against Israel? Gog is called the chief prince. Earlier, we concluded that a prince is an angel, but we now focus our attention on the *chief* prince or chief angel. The word *chief* in Hebrew is the word *Rosh,* which means *the head.* Many believe Russia is *Rosh* or the head leader of the coalition that invades Israel. They have taken this position because scripture states that the chief prince or head travels from the north of Israel. Russia is not the only nation located north of Israel. There are several nations north of Israel, and they are Lebanon, Syria, and Turkey.

> Dan. 11:43   But he shall have power over the treasures of gold and of silver, and over all the precious things of Egypt: and the Libyans and the Ethiopians *shall be* at his steps.
>
> Dan. 11:44   But tidings out of the east and out of the north shall trouble him: therefore he shall go forth with great fury to destroy, and utterly to make away many.

Assuming Russia is the leader of the invading coalition from the north of Israel, then based on the book of Daniel, it will be Russia that will also have an enemy just north of her borders. That means Russia will also have an enemy on two fronts. Scripture tells us that the enemy to the south is Israel, but what country is north of Russia? There are no countries north of Russia; therefore, we have to rule out Russia as the coalition's leader invading Israel in the last days.

> Eze. 38:3   And say, Thus saith the Lord GOD; Behold, I *am* against thee, O Gog, the chief prince of Meshech and Tubal:
>
> Eze. 38:4   And I will turn thee back, and put hooks into thy jaws, and I will bring thee forth, and all thine army, horses and horsemen, all of them clothed with all sorts *of armour, even* a great company *with* bucklers and shields, all of them handling swords:
>
> Eze. 38:5   Persia, Ethiopia, and Libya with them; all of them with shield and helmet:
>
> Eze. 38:6   Gomer, and all his bands; the house of Togarmah of the north quarters, and all his bands: *and* many people with thee.

Earlier, we identified Magog as the land or territory over which Gog reigns. The name of that territory is Meshech and Tubal. Scripture identifies some of the nations that will join together to form the land of Magog. Those nations are Persia, Ethiopia, Libya, Gomer, and Togarmah. All of these countries make up the coalition of Magog that comes to fight against Israel. Magog is the spiritual or sacred name of that coalition, and Meshech and Tubal are the physical or formal names of the alliance. Persia is present-day Iran. Ethiopia and Libya are off the eastern and northern coasts of Africa. Scripture states, this coalition will come from the north of Israel. Today there aren't any nations that are north of Israel with the name of Gomer and Togarmah. At the time Ezekiel wrote this prophecy, the names of these nations were different.

Gen. 10:1   Now these *are* the generations of the sons of Noah, Shem, Ham, and Japheth: and unto them were sons born after the flood.

Gen. 10:2   The sons of Japheth; Gomer, and Magog, and Madai, and Javan, and Tubal, and Meshech, and Tiras.

Gen. 10:3   And the sons of Gomer; Ashkenaz, and Riphath, and Togarmah.

Let's examine scripture to discover the true identity of the leader of the invading coalition. Some of the members of the alliance that comes from the north and invade Israel in the latter days are Meshech, Tubal, Gomer, and Togarmah. Noah's sons are Shem, Ham, and Japheth, and the sons of Japheth are Gomer, Tubal, and Meshech. One of Gomer's son's name is Togarmah. Ezekiel prophesied that these nations would invade Israel in the latter days. By today's standards, all of these unrecognizable names are descendants of Japheth, who settled in a region north of Israel. Ezekiel 38:6 states, "Gomer, and all his bands; the house of Togarmah of the north quarters, and all his bands." This region is identifiable as Asia Minor, which is modern-day Turkey. Russia will not lead the coalition against Israel. The nation of Turkey will be the head or leader of this coalition.

Utilizing the Jewish Study Bible, some maps in the back show the regions where Noah's sons settled after the flood. Noah's three sons are Shem, Ham, and Japheth. The only son to homestead north of Israel is Japheth, and he settled in a region just south of the Black Sea. This particular area is modern-day Turkey, and the following names Meshech, Tubal, Gomer, and Togarmah, are listed right there on the map.

The War

Eze. 39:1 Therefore, thou son of man, prophesy against Gog, and say, Thus saith the Lord GOD; Behold, I *am* against thee, O Gog, the chief prince of Meshech and Tubal:

Eze. 39:2 And I will turn thee back, and leave but the sixth part of thee, and will cause thee to come up from the north parts, and will bring thee upon the mountains of Israel:

Eze. 39:3 And I will smite thy bow out of thy left hand, and will cause thine arrows to fall out of thy right hand.

Eze. 39:4 Thou shalt fall upon the mountains of Israel, thou, and all thy bands, and the people that *is* with thee: I will give thee unto the ravenous birds of every sort, and *to* the beasts of the field to be devoured.

Eze. 39:5 Thou shalt fall upon the open field: for I have spoken *it*, saith the Lord GOD.

The Battle of Armageddon is a one-battle war and a one-sided battle. The enemy of God will never have a chance. The enemy marches into the mountains of Israel, where he will meet his demise. The armies of God will deliver a crushing defeat to Gog and Magog by killing five out of six of all their military personnel.

The Post War Feast

Eze. 39:17   And, thou son of man, thus saith the Lord
GOD; Speak unto every feathered fowl, and to
every beast of the field, Assemble yourselves,
and come; gather yourselves on every side to
my sacrifice that I do sacrifice for you, *even* a
great sacrifice upon the mountains of Israel,
that ye may eat flesh, and drink blood.

Eze. 39:18   Ye shall eat the flesh of the mighty, and drink
the blood of the princes of the earth, of rams,
of lambs, and of goats, of bullocks, all of them
fatlings of Bashan.

Eze. 39:19   And ye shall eat fat till ye be full, and drink
blood till ye be drunken, of my sacrifice which
I have sacrificed for you.

Eze. 39:20   Thus ye shall be filled at my table with horses
and chariots, with mighty men, and with all
men of war, saith the Lord GOD.

After the completion of the Battle of Armageddon, there
will be a great feast on the mountains of Israel. The remains of
the soldiers killed in the Battle of Armageddon become a
smorgasbord for all of the birds of the air and the beasts of the
field. The flesh of the dead soldiers will be equivalent to a
sacrifice or sin offering. Instead of the sacrifice being rams and
goats, the offering will consist of the soldiers' flesh, and the
drink offering will be their blood.

The great feast in the mountains of Israel is the Marriage
Supper of the Lamb. Revelation 19:9 states, "Blessed are they
which are called unto the Marriage Supper of the Lamb." The
Marriage Supper of the Lamb is not a dining experience for the
resurrected saints. The guests dining at the Marriage Supper
aren't the saints. The saints will be the servants, and the guests
will be the birds of the air and the beasts of the field. The cuisine
that the saints serve at the Marriage Supper is the army of Gog
and Magog. The saints and the animals are blessed because both
play a significant role in the Lamb's Marriage Supper. The saints

get to serve all of God's enemies as a smorgasbord to the animals, and they will dine until they are full.

> Rev. 19:17 And I saw an angel standing in the sun; and he cried with a loud voice, saying to all the fowls that fly in the midst of heaven, Come and gather yourselves together unto the supper of the great God;
>
> Rev. 19:18 That ye may eat the flesh of kings, and the flesh of captains, and the flesh of mighty men, and the flesh of horses, and of them that sit on them, and the flesh of all *men, both* free and bond, both small and great.

The supper of the great God is the Marriage Supper of the Lamb. The supper of the great God is when the animals will eat the flesh of kings, the flesh of soldiers, and the flesh of other animals. After the Marriage Supper, the saints will partake in another celebration. They will enter into the New Jerusalem, and there they will eat fruit from the Tree of Life. Revelation 22:14 states, "That they may have right to the tree of life, and may enter in through the gates into the city." They will also be allowed to eat manna. Revelation 2:17 states, "To him that overcometh will I give to eat of the hidden manna." The food at the Lamb's Marriage Supper is very different from what the saints are partaking. The Marriage Supper of the Lamb is a one-time meal prepared for the animals, and the cuisine consists of the flesh of the defeated soldiers. The food of which the saints will dine is manna and fruit from the Tree of Life. These are spiritual foods, and the saints will partake of them forever.

Post-War Cleanup

> Eze. 39:8 Behold, it is come, and it is done, saith the Lord GOD; this *is* the day whereof I have spoken.

Eze. 39:9   And they that dwell in the cities of Israel shall go forth, and shall set on fire and burn the weapons, both the shields and the bucklers, the bows and the arrows, and the handstaves, and the spears, and they shall burn them with fire seven years:

Eze. 39:10   So that they shall take no wood out of the field, neither cut down *any* out of the forests; for they shall burn the weapons with fire: and they shall spoil those that spoiled them, and rob those that robbed them, saith the Lord GOD.

Eze. 39:11   And it shall come to pass in that day, *that* I will give unto Gog a place there of graves in Israel, the valley of the passengers on the east of the sea: and it shall stop the *noses* of the passengers: and there shall they bury Gog and all his multitude: and they shall call *it* The valley of Hamongog.

Eze. 39:12   And seven months shall the house of Israel be burying of them, that they may cleanse the land.

Eze. 39:13   Yea, all the people of the land shall bury *them*, and it shall be to them a renown the day that I shall be glorified, saith the Lord GOD.

After the enemy is defeated, then comes the post-war era. Now it's time to bury all the dead to prevent sickness and disease. It's time to care for the wounded and rid the nation of any signs of the war. The first order of business is to bury the dead, but first, they search the bodies to confiscate any money, gold, jewelry, or other valuables to be preserved. Once they seize the fallen soldiers' spoils, they bury the dead in mass graves. There are so many dead that it will take at least seven months before locating all the dead and burying them.

The next order for cleansing the land is to remove all the military equipment that was left behind. The amount of weaponry was so vast that it would take seven years to purge it all. The weapons will also contain unburned oil, and they stockpile it for fuel. Israel will not have to cut down any trees for fuel for seven years because of all the petroleum products they confiscated from the tanks, planes, helicopters, etc. These seven years are not in the *Tribulation Period*, but they are the first seven years of the Millennium. It's not the saints that will be using this fuel, but the left-behind mortals will use it. These are the individuals that the saints will rule and reign over for one thousand years. Revelation 5:10 states, "And hast made us unto our God kings and priests: and we shall reign on the earth."

When comparing the battle described in Revelation 16:16-21 and the war described in Ezekiel 38:20-23, we see they are the same battle. Both wars take place during the End-times, and both consist of hail, fire, and brimstone. After both wars, humanity magnifies God's name from that day forward. Furthermore, Ezekiel 39:8 and Revelation 16:17 contains the same phrase after these great battles; *it is done.*

Armageddon's Battleground

Eze. 39:4   Thou shalt fall upon the mountains of Israel, thou, and all thy bands, and the people that *is* with thee: I will give thee unto the ravenous birds of every sort, and *to* the beasts of the field to be devoured.

Joe. 2:20   But I will remove far off from you the northern *army*, and will drive him into a land barren and desolate, with his face toward the east sea, and his hinder part toward the utmost sea, and his stink shall come up, and his ill savour shall come up, because he hath done great things.

Strategic locations are the scene of many significant battles. Many military generals strategically steer their adversaries into a specific area to establish a final stronghold. They chose these locations because his military will enjoys a significant advantage over his counterpart. Because Jerusalem is the objective, it's ironic that this battle should occur in the mountains of Israel. Gog and Magog positions themselves within Israel's borders, between the Mediterranean Sea to the west and the Dead Sea and Sea of Galilee to the east. Ultimately, Gog and Magog will come to their end, on the outskirts of the Holy City. Ironically, such an immense sacrifice takes place in the shadows of Jerusalem. The deceased and decaying bodies' stench is comparable to an odor of a sweet smell like the rising smoke of a burnt offering (Exo. 29:18). The odor of a sweet smell is synonymous with the prayers of the saints (Rev. 5:8). Note, at the Battle of Armageddon, the inhabitants of Israel and the saints just received an answer to their prayers.

CHAPTER 10

THE EUPHRATES RIVER

Rev. 16:12   And the sixth angel poured out his vial upon the great river Euphrates; and the water thereof was dried up, that the way of the kings of the east might be prepared.

Rev. 16:13   And I saw three unclean spirits like frogs come out of the mouth of the dragon, and out of the mouth of the beast, and out of the mouth of the false prophet.

Rev. 16:14   For they are the spirits of devils, working miracles, which go forth unto the kings of the earth and of the whole world, to gather them to the battle of that great day of God Almighty.

Rev. 16:15   Behold, I come as a thief. Blessed is he that watcheth, and keepeth his garments, lest he walk naked, and they see his shame.

Rev. 16:16   And he gathered them together into a place called in the Hebrew tongue Armageddon.

IN the End-times, the outpouring of the sixth vial of God's Wrath establishes a super hi-way for the kings of the east because the Euphrates River will dry up. The drying up of the Euphrates River creates an avenue that provides direct access to the nation of Israel for the Battle of Armageddon. The kings from the east have a vast army consisting of two hundred million soldiers massed and poised while waiting for military orders to attack Israel. Such an enormous army demands a significant thoroughfare for transportation and logistics. Once the waters of the Euphrates River are dried up, the dry riverbed is used as a mode of transportation.

Whenever the topic of the Euphrates River surfaces, attention is automatically focused on the river positioned a few hundred miles northeast of the nation of Israel. That is the only major river with that name. The Euphrates River flows through the countries of Turkey, Syria, and Iraq. Scripture affirms the fact that the Battle of Armageddon takes place within the borders of Israel. Most scholars have determined the scene of this great battle to be at Megiddo in the Jezreel Valley of Israel. Please note, the Euphrates River and the Battle of Armageddon at Megiddo in the Jezreel Valley does not compute, according to the facts. Even with the Euphrates River drying up, it is still hundreds of miles away from Megiddo, Israel. If this mega-army have to travel from the Euphrates River, it will be a long-drawn-out march to Israel and will take weeks or even months before they arrive. Remember, God's Wrath is already in session. The Battle of Armageddon will occur at the outpouring of the sixth of the seven vials of God's Wrath. The first five vials of His Wrath has already begun. God's judgment is swift and just, indicating the Euphrates River referenced in this instance is not the conventional Euphrates River. It would have to be a river located near or within Israel's borders with the same name. Please note, the known or established Euphrates River doesn't flow anywhere near the nation of Israel.

Let's take a look at the definition of Euphrates. The Strong's number for *Euphrates* is #H6578, and it means *a river of the east*. What river is on the eastern border of Israel? The Jordan River is Israel's eastern border. To minimize the possibility of confusion, when referencing the Euphrates River that flows through Turkey, Syria, and Iraq, the phrase *conventional Euphrates River* will be used to differentiate between the two.

The following scriptures reference a river named the Euphrates. Accompanying each verse or range of verses is a possible explanation that gives more insight into how the phrases River Euphrates or Euphrates River is relevant to Israel.

> Gen. 2:8   And the LORD God planted a garden eastward in Eden; and there he put the man whom he had formed.
>
> Gen. 2:9   And out of the ground made the LORD God to grow every tree that is pleasant to the sight, and good for food; the tree of life also in the midst of the garden, and the tree of knowledge of good and evil.

Gen. 2:10   And a river went out of Eden to water the garden; and from thence it was parted, and became into four heads.

Gen. 2:11   The name of the first is Pison: that is it which compasseth the whole land of Havilah, where there is gold;

Gen. 2:12   And the gold of that land is good: there is bdellium and the onyx stone.

Gen. 2:13   And the name of the second river is Gihon: the same is it that compasseth the whole land of Ethiopia.

Gen. 2:14   And the name of the third river is Hiddekel: that is it which goeth toward the east of Assyria. And the fourth river is Euphrates.

Where is the Euphrates River Located?

Many debates have taken place about the actual location of the Garden of Eden. The Garden of Eden formed four rivers, and the Euphrates River was one of them. These conversations center on the fact that the conventional Euphrates River was always one of the main focal points in deciding the location of the Garden of Eden. Some scholars believed the Garden of Eden is in the Persian Gulf region, because of its proximity to the Hiddekel River, which is the Tigris River. The Euphrates Rivers and the Tigris River flows parallel to each other until they intersect in that region. Perhaps we've been looking at the wrong Euphrates River. The fourth river, that's named the Euphrates River, could be the river on Israel's eastern border (Jordan River) rather than the conventional Euphrates River. If the Euphrates River is the eastern border of Israel, then that narrows the location of the Garden of Eden to an area in the vicinity of the Promised Land.

Gen. 15:18 In the same day the LORD made a covenant with Abram, saying, Unto thy seed have I given this land, from the river of Egypt unto the great river, the river Euphrates:

Israel's Borders

Genesis 15:18 is referencing Israel's southern and eastern borders. Israel's southern border is shared with Egypt, while her eastern boundary is the Jordan River. The nation of Israel is also called the Promised Land, formerly known as Canaan Land. The Children of Israel entered into the Promised Land as they crossed over a river on the eastern border of Canaan Land. That river was the Jordan River. Israel's original borders never included the conventional Euphrates River. Israel's eastern border is the Jordan River, the river on the east, as per the *Euphrates'* definition.

> Deu. 1:7   Turn you, and take your journey, and go to the mount of the Amorites, and unto all the places nigh thereunto, in the plain, in the hills, and in the vale, and in the south, and by the sea side, to the land of the Canaanites, and unto Lebanon, unto the great river, the river Euphrates.

Deuteronomy 1:7 is referencing Moses leading the Children of Israel through the wilderness on their way to the Promised Land. Moses led them just south of the Dead Sea and along the eastern border of the Dead Sea, up to the Jordan River's eastern shore. Once they crossed over the Jordan River, they were in the Promised Land. Moses never led them anywhere near the conventional Euphrates River.

> Deu. 11:24 Every place whereon the soles of your feet shall tread shall be yours: from the wilderness and Lebanon, from the river, the river Euphrates, even unto the uttermost sea shall your coast be.

God promised the twelve tribes of Israel all the land between the Jordan River on the east and the Mediterranean Sea to the west. The northern border extended to Lebanon and Israel shares the southern border with Egypt. If Israel's easternmost boundary is the conventional Euphrates River, they would have already been in the Promised Land long before crossing the Jordan River. Yes, Israel did have two and a half tribes on the Jordan River's eastern shore, but that wasn't a part of the Promised Land. God allowed them to possess that land, but it wasn't a part of the original agreement.

> Jos. 1:4   From the wilderness and this Lebanon even unto the great river, the river Euphrates, all the land of the Hittites, and unto the great sea toward the going down of the sun, shall be your coast.

Joshua 1:4 is another reference to the borders of Israel. Israel's borders encompass all of the lands between the Jordan River on the east and the Mediterranean Sea on the west. The land of the Hittites is a remnant of the Promised Land (Exo. 3:8). In this case, the Euphrates River refers to the Jordan River, the eastern border of the Promised Land, and it is not a reference to the conventional Euphrates River.

> 2Sa. 8:3   David smote also Hadadezer, the son of Rehob, king of Zobah, as he went to recover his border at the river Euphrates.

> 1Ch. 18:3   And David smote Hadarezer king of Zobah unto Hamath, as he went to stablish his dominion by the river Euphrates.

Zobah is a place near Ammon, Edom, and Moab, which is in the vicinity of the Dead Sea and Jordan River. David reclaimed his borders in this region, which are Israel's eastern borders. The conventional Euphrates River is hundreds of miles from Zobah.

> 2Ki. 23:29   In his days Pharaohnechoh king of Egypt went up against the king of Assyria to the river Euphrates: and king Josiah went against him; and he slew him at Megiddo, when he had seen him.

The Euphrates River and Megiddo

Here we have the River Euphrates and Megiddo seemingly at the same site. Again, the conventional Euphrates River does not flow through Israel, and Megiddo's location is in the Jezreel Valley of Israel. It's impossible for a king or any person, for that matter, to be in two different places at the same time. For that reason, this reference to the Euphrates River is a river within Israel's borders, or perhaps it forms one of Israel's borders.

Armed with this information, we can launch a search for clarity and a better understanding of the Euphrates River's actual location. The research begins with establishing Euphrates' real meaning, both in the Greek and the Hebrew languages. According to Strong's Greek Dictionary, the definition of *Euphrates* is #G2166, and it means *a river in Asia.* The Strong's Hebrew meaning of Euphrates' is #H6578, and it means *a river of the East.* At first glance, this information does not seem to be relevant. Upon closer examination of Israel's rivers, the river on the east may be perhaps the eastern border of Israel, the Jordan River. The definition of Euphrates fits because the Jordan River is the easternmost boundary of Israel. If the Jordan River is, in fact, the Euphrates River, regarding the Battle of Armageddon, then all the pieces of the puzzle begin to fit. As the Euphrates River (Jordan River) dries up, it will form a significant thoroughfare providing direct and immediate access within Israel's borders. This information eliminates all barriers that previously hindered such a large army's direct access within Israel's borders. Now the kings' army from the east can march right across the dry riverbed into neighboring Israel. This plan is very strategic because Israel will have a two hundred-million-man army invading her borders on two different fronts. A portion of the military will invade from the north (Joe. 2:20) while the remainder of the army will flank from the east by way of the Euphrates River (Jordan River).

> 2Ki. 24:7   And the king of Egypt came not again any more out of his land: for the king of Babylon had taken

from the river of Egypt unto the river Euphrates
all that pertained to the king of Egypt.

According to the preceding verse, the land around the
conventional Euphrates River is already a possession of the King
of Babylon. The conquered land in 2 Kings 24:7 is the land in the
Jordan River or Israel's eastern boundary. The timing of Babylon
confiscating Egypt is about the same time that King
Nebuchadnezzar is preparing to conquer Judah and take the
captives back to Babylon, thereby indicating the location of the
Euphrates River is in the vicinity of the Jordan River.

> 1Ch. 5:9   And eastward he inhabited unto the entering in
> of the wilderness from the river Euphrates:
> because their cattle were multiplied in the land of
> Gilead.

1 Chronicles 5:9 is a reference to the inheritance of the tribe
of Reuben. Note, Reuben, Gad, and half of the tribe of Manasseh
inherited land east of the Jordan River (Jos.18:7). Reuben's western
border was the Jordan River, which is also the eastern border of
Israel. Reuben's land extended eastward from the Jordan River, but
even Reuben's land did not extend to the conventional Euphrates
River.

> 2Ch. 35:20 After all this, when Josiah had prepared the
> temple, Necho king of Egypt came up to fight
> against Carchemish by Euphrates: and Josiah
> went out against him.

> Jer. 46:2   Against Egypt, against the army of Pharaohnecho
> king of Egypt, which was by the river Euphrates
> in Carchemish, which Nebuchadrezzar king of
> Babylon smote in the fourth year of Jehoiakim
> the son of Josiah king of Judah.

Carchemish is the natives of Chemosh, a place located near
Moab and Ammon, which lies off the coast of the Jordan River.
There was a battle between the King of Babylon and the King of

Egypt. King Josiah of Judah interfered with the King of Egypt, and as a result, he died in that war. Note the fighting in this battle took place at Megiddo, which isn't anywhere near the conventional Euphrates River. This information indicates the Euphrates River is a river located in Israel or nearby vicinity. Substituting Euphrates' definition (a river of the east) could refer to the Jordan River because it is the easternmost river in Israel.

Jer. 13:4	Take the girdle that thou hast got, which is upon thy loins, and arise, go to Euphrates, and hide it there in a hole of the rock.
Jer. 13:5	So I went, and hid it by Euphrates, as the LORD commanded me.
Jer. 13:6	And it came to pass after many days, that the LORD said unto me, Arise, go to Euphrates, and take the girdle from thence, which I commanded thee to hide there.
Jer. 13:7	Then I went to Euphrates, and digged, and took the girdle from the place where I had hid it: and, behold, the girdle was marred, it was profitable for nothing.

Jeremiah and the Euphrates River

Jeremiah was a descendant of the tribe of Benjamin, and he lived in the town of Anathoth, near the Jordan River. The Lord instructed Jeremiah to hide a girdle at the Euphrates River. The definition of Euphrates is the river on the east or perhaps the Jordan River. It's inconceivable to think that God would tell Jeremiah to go to the conventional Euphrates River, which is hundreds of miles away and located in a foreign country, to hide something that pertains to Israel. The Jordan River (the river of the east) is right there near his home. The girdle that Jeremiah hid was a garment worn on one's loins. The procreation of life comes from the loins; therefore, it was to demonstrate Israel's heart condition or mindset. Eventually, Jeremiah retrieved the garment.

Upon retrieval of the girdle, he noticed the girdle had begun to decay. The symbolism is to show the relationship between God and the Children of Israel was deteriorating. Again, it is conceivable to think the location of the Euphrates is within the borders of Israel because destruction originates from within.

Jer. 51:63   And it shall be, when thou hast made an end of reading this book, that thou shalt bind a stone to it, and cast it into the midst of Euphrates:

Jeremiah was a prophet of Israel, and God gave Jeremiah detailed information about the fall of Babylon. Just as God gave Jeremiah instructions to place the girdle near the Euphrates River, The Lord also instructed him to throw a book of prophecy into the Euphrates River. The book contained a prediction about the fate of Babylon, but it was not to warn Babylon. It was a revelation to Israel that one day Babylon, who placed Judah in bondage, will also suffer destruction. Because the purpose of the prophecy was for Israel, then it stands to reason that the book is hidden somewhere in Israel's vicinity and not at the conventional Euphrates River. Please note, the prophecy was favorable for Israel, meaning that after the destruction of Babylon, the Israelites would return to their native land by crossing the Euphrates River (Jordan River).

Jer. 46:6   Let not the swift flee away, nor the mighty man escape; they shall stumble, and fall toward the north by the river Euphrates.

Jer. 46:10   For this is the day of the Lord GOD of hosts, a day of vengeance, that he may avenge him of his adversaries: and the sword shall devour, and it shall be satiate and made drunk with their blood: for the Lord GOD of hosts hath a sacrifice in the north country by the river Euphrates.

The Battle of Armageddon at the Euphrates River

These verses are referencing the Battle of Armageddon or the day of the Lord. We know the Battle of Armageddon occurs within Israel's borders, and it is immediately after the saints receive their new spiritual bodies. The Battle of Armageddon is the Day of the Lord and when God punishes the non-believers who openly reject Him by directly challenging His deity. Before His death, Jesus promised born-again believers immortality, but they continued to live in a mortal body. Just before the Battle of Armageddon, born-again believers will enter into that promise of immortality. The saints will receive their new spiritual bodies. Those bodies are exactly like the body Christ possessed after His resurrection. Immediately after rewarding the saints with immortality, the Lord dispenses His Wrath, and the Battle of Armageddon is a remnant of that Wrath.

The Battle of Armageddon is comparable to a blood sacrifice. It parallels with the fact that there must be bloodshed before the forgiveness of sins. Hebrews 9:22 states, "Almost all things are by the law purged with blood and without shedding of blood is no remission." Something else to consider, all blood sacrifices must take place at a place that God chooses (Due 16:2). God chose a location within the borders of Israel because Israel is where God has established His name. Judges. 21:19 points out that the first place where Israel began to hold their appointed sacrifices was in Shiloh, which is well inside Israel's borders. The location of Shiloh is another strong indication that the reference to the Euphrates River is alluding to a river in Israel and not the conventional Euphrates River.

Rev. 9:14   Saying to the sixth angel which had the trumpet, Loose the four angels which are bound in the great river Euphrates.

Rev. 16:12   And the sixth angel poured out his vial upon the great river Euphrates; and the water thereof was dried up, that the way of the kings of the east might be prepared.

These verses are referencing the two hundred million-man-army stationed on the Euphrates River during the End-times. Revelation 9:14 shows a strategically positioned army, but four angels detained them. Likewise, Revelation 16:12 is referencing the same event, only now the Great River Euphrates is being dried up. When it dries up, it will provide a major thoroughfare, leading directly into Israel, so that the two hundred million-man-army can blaze a path of destruction within Israel's borders. Scripture also affirms that the Battle of Armageddon will occur in Israel; therefore, this cannot be the conventional Euphrates River. This reference to the Euphrates River must be referencing a river in Israel with the same name or description. Euphrates' Hebrew meaning (a river on the east) and the enormous army's location are synonymous with the Jordan River. This army is preparing an invasion of Israel, and it will be coming from the east across the Jordan River, which is the easternmost border of Israel.

This information is strong evidence that the Jordan River is the Euphrates River, concerning the Battle of Armageddon. One problem is solved, but another one is born. The situation now is that Megiddo, Israel, isn't anywhere near the Jordan River. This fact prompts another word search for the meaning of the word Armageddon. This word consists of two Hebrew words, which are *har* and *megiddon*. According to Strong's Greek Dictionary, *har* is #H2022, and it means a mountain or range of hills, and *Megiddon* is #H1413, which means rendezvous. Combining the meanings of the two words yields a different sense of understanding. Armageddon means a pre-determined meeting on a mountain or range of hills. Fortified with this information, the Battle of Armageddon does not have to occur at Megiddo, Israel. Because Armageddon is a rendezvous point, the battle can take place almost anywhere within Israel's borders at a pre-determined time and a pre-determined location. Only The Lord knows that specific time and place. The only criteria concerning the site of the Battle of Armageddon is that it must occur within Israel's borders and near a mountain range. The conventional Euphrates River does not meet this criteria, but the Jordan River matches perfectly. Isaiah

14:25 states, "That I will break the Assyrian in my land, and upon my mountains tread him under foot: then shall his yoke depart from off them, and his burden depart from off their shoulders." All the information seems to point to the fact that The Euphrates River is the Jordan River.

CHAPTER 11

THE BRIDE OF CHRIST

A royal wedding is a marriage of royalty, such as a king, queen, prince, etc. In the real world, any marriage can have the classification of a royal wedding, but in the grand scheme of things, there is only one royal wedding, and that is the marriage of Jesus Christ, our Lord and Savior.

Just as in traditional marriages, there are also specific qualifications that must be present before a groom and his bride can be joined in a royal wedding of holy matrimony. Not just anybody qualifies for that honor. Either the groom or the bride will have to be born into the royal family. The person of royalty must choose a spouse to complete the second half of that union. If one is not a descendant of a royal family, they cannot have a royal wedding unless the royal bride or royal groom chooses him or her for their hand in marriage. The potential spouse selected by the royal family member must undergo extreme background scrutiny, and it must be verifiable. This verification process is synonymous with God's requirements for the participants in a heavenly wedding.

The royal family is the ruling family of a kingdom. The ruling family's descendants automatically qualify as heirs; however, the throne has limitations to the firstborn only. In the heavenly wedding, the domain is the entire world, and the king is God. Since Jesus is the only begotten Son of God; therefore, He is the sole heir. He has the authority to choose whomsoever He desires to be His bride.

Qualifications

Mat. 1:21   And she shall bring forth a son, and thou shalt call his name JESUS: for he shall save his people from their sins.

Mat. 1:22   Now all this was done, that it might be fulfilled which was spoken of the Lord by the prophet, saying,

Mat. 1:23   Behold, a virgin shall be with child, and shall bring forth a son, and they shall call his name Emmanuel, which being interpreted is, God with us.

Usually, in a traditional royal wedding, the heirs' names aren't known until they are born. In the case of the heavenly marriage, everyone knows the successor before-hand. Isaiah prophesied it several centuries earlier. Isaiah 7:14 states, "The Lord himself shall give you a sign; Behold, a virgin shall conceive, and bear a son, and shall call his name Immanuel." Although Jesus' name was not Immanuel, the prophecy was still referencing Him. The name Immanuel becomes apparent in the gospels. Matthew 1:23 states, "Behold, a virgin shall be with child, and shall bring forth a son, and they shall call his name Emmanuel, which being interpreted is, God with us." Emmanuel (Immanuel) has two different spellings because one spelling is Hebrew and the other spelling in Greek. Notice, Matthew 1:23 gives the meaning of Immanuel. It means *God with us,* and that became apparent with the birth of Jesus. He, being God, began to dwell with humanity (Joh. 1:14).

Prophecy indicates that His name was Emmanuel, but what does that have to do with Jesus? An angel came to Joseph and told him that Mary would give birth to a son, and his name was to be called Jesus. On the surface, this appears to be a contradiction, but the focus is not on the name of Jesus, The main focal point is that Mary was a virgin, and her son is the Son of God. Jesus is her son's name. He was born on earth, and He lived on earth. That was a fulfillment of the prophecy given many years earlier. Isaiah prophesied that a virgin shall have a son, and He shall be called Emmanuel. The name Emmanuel means *God with us.* When Jesus came into the world, that is what happened; He was the Son of God, living as a human being with us on earth.

Rev. 5:5   And one of the elders saith unto me, Weep not: behold, the Lion of the tribe of Juda, the Root of David, hath prevailed to open the book, and to loose the seven seals thereof.

According to the prophecy, it was inevitable that the groom's name is Jesus. He must be a descendant of the tribe of Judah, and His lineage must be of the root and offspring of David, the king of Israel. Jesus' origin can be traced back to David from His mother's side, and it can be traced by to David on His stepfather's side of the family. Jesus' ancestry from Joseph's side is in Matthew 1:1-16. Jesus' genealogy from His mother's side is in Luke 3:23-38. Contrary to popular belief, Jesus' parents were married at the time the Holy Spirit overshadowed her with a child; otherwise, Jesus would have been born out of wedlock, which is a violation of God's law. Matthew 1:19 states that Joseph was Mary's husband.

Heb. 4:15   For we have not an high priest which cannot be touched with the feeling of our infirmities; but was in all points tempted like as *we are, yet* without sin.

Because this will be a heavenly wedding, there's one more qualification that's essential, and only one person in the entire world is qualified for that role. That one qualification was to be sin-free. Mary, being a human being, gave birth to Jesus; therefore, He was automatically born with a death sentence due to the sin of Adam and Eve. Jesus' birth was the result of His mother's immaculate conception by the Holy Spirit; therefore, He did not succumb to the ways of this world. Jesus' lifestyle pleased God because He was only motivated by the Spirit of His Father and not by the will of His flesh. Furthermore, He was tempted in all points, just as man undergoes temptation. The difference is, He remained faithful to the Spirit that comes from His Father and rejects the lusts of the flesh, rendering Him a sinless individual.

Joh. 3:3   Jesus answered and said unto him, Verily, verily, I say unto thee, Except a man be born again, he cannot see the kingdom of God.

In a traditional royal wedding, the non-royal member's qualifications are entirely dependent upon the member of the royal family's choice. There are a wide variety of reasons for choosing a particular individual. The reasons range from love, beauty, compatibility, political gains, etc. In the heavenly wedding, the qualifications for the bride is that she must be born again. It has nothing to do with beauty, financial status, political gains, religious gain, etc. It is strictly dependent upon an individual's relationship with Jesus, the Son of God.

The Location of the Kingdom

> Joh. 1:13   Which were born, not of blood, nor of the will of
>   the flesh, nor of the will of man, but of God.

Every kingdom has a domain or territory over which the king reigns. In the case of the heavenly wedding, the kingdom is heaven and earth. Jesus qualified for both of these domains. He was born of the Spirit, which declares Him to be the Son of God, and He was also born of a woman; that makes Him the Son of man; therefore, He is the only candidate with jurisdiction in heaven and on earth.

Usually, in a traditional royal wedding, neither party will be of alien descent. In conventional royal weddings, sometimes, the royal family chooses a spouse from another country but never chooses a spouse from another planet. Jesus' Father was God, which was from heaven, and His mother was an earthly being. Jesus will choose a bride from the earth; therefore, one can classify His bride as being of alien descent.

The Betrothal Period

> Mat. 24:13   But he that shall endure unto the end, the same
>   shall be saved.

In a traditional royal wedding, the assumption is for the spouse-elect is to remain faithful right up to the time the groom returns for the wedding. That's also the case in the heavenly wedding because being born-again is equivalent to a marriage proposal. Just because someone gets engaged, that does not guarantee that a marriage will result from that engagement. The spouse-elect in a heavenly wedding must also remain faithful to the groom while waiting for His return. In other words, if the spouse-elect does not practice abstinence, then she can be rejected before the wedding ceremony.

The Wedding Attire

Mat. 22:11   And when the king came in to see the guests, he saw there a man which had not on a wedding garment:

Mat. 22:12   And he saith unto him, Friend, how camest thou in hither not having a wedding garment? And he was speechless.

Mat. 22:13   Then said the king to the servants, Bind him hand and foot, and take him away, and cast *him* into outer darkness; there shall be weeping and gnashing of teeth.

As in any wedding, the bride and groom should wear the proper attire. Usually, the groom wears a tuxedo, and the bride wears a gown. There is no set color of the groom's tuxedo, but the bride's dress is white more often than not. White is a symbolic gesture that the future bride is pure and has adequately prepared herself to enter holy matrimony. This same principle is true concerning a heavenly wedding. The bride's wedding attire is white because the color white is the metaphorical color of righteousness (Rev. 19:8).

Rev. 19:7   Let us be glad and rejoice, and give honour to him: for the marriage of the Lamb is come, and his wife hath made herself ready.

Rev. 19:8   And to her was granted that she should be
             arrayed in fine linen, clean and white: for the fine
             linen is the righteousness of saints.

The wedding attire in a heavenly wedding must be white
because white represents the righteousness of the saints. Not only
are they to be white, but they must also be clean. In other words,
the expectation is to minimize infractions against the covenant
while waiting for the wedding. Even though the spouse-elect is
born-again, he or she must continually seek forgiveness for minor
offenses. Requesting forgiveness is in no way indicating that one
should repent repeatedly. Repenting is changing the way you think
or aligning your thoughts with God's word. Once an individual
repents, that person will continually make minor adjustments to
maintain a righteous lifestyle as they travel the straight and narrow
road leading to everlasting life. Making small changes to support a
godly lifestyle is the meaning of the phrase *endure until the end.*
Making minor adjustments is in no way indicating that a spouse-
elect had been unfaithful, but it is preparing oneself mentally for
married life.

The Invited Guests

Rev. 7:9   After this I beheld, and, lo, a great multitude,
             which no man could number, of all nations, and
             kindreds, and people, and tongues, stood before
             the throne, and before the Lamb, clothed with
             white robes, and palms in their hands;
Rev. 7:10   And cried with a loud voice, saying, Salvation to
             our God which sitteth upon the throne, and unto
             the Lamb.
Rev. 7:11   And all the angels stood round about the throne,
             and *about* the elders and the four beasts, and fell
             before the throne on their faces, and worshipped
             God,

Rev. 7:12   Saying, Amen: Blessing, and glory, and wisdom, and thanksgiving, and honour, and power, and might, *be* unto our God for ever and ever. Amen.

Every wedding has guests. The royal wedding will also have guests. The guests at the heavenly wedding will be more distinguished than any of the guests attending the grandest of traditional weddings. It will consist of elders, angels, and other celestial beings. The officiating priest in the heavenly wedding will be God himself. What God joins together is not unequally yoked; therefore, it cannot fail. It is a marriage made in heaven.

The Wedding Vows

Rev. 21:4   And God shall wipe away all tears from their eyes; and there shall be no more death, neither sorrow, nor crying, neither shall there be any more pain: for the former things are passed away.

In the wedding ceremony, the bride and groom mutually vow to be joined together as one and will only be separated by death. A promise of this magnitude is insinuating that the marriage will last forever. The same principle applies to a heavenly wedding, except that both parties are immune from death. The divine wedding is positively and truly an eternal marriage because Almighty God ordains this union.

Vows that join two individuals for life seemingly indicate that the word divorce is non-existent. Please note, many royal marriages still end up in divorce, even after declaring such vows. Divorce happens because either the bride, the groom began to allow outside influences to enter their lives. Outside influences introduce friction into the marriage, which ultimately leads to separation or divorce. Many marriages end up in divorce for just about any reason under the sun. Although there is a high percentage of divorces, that wasn't God's original plan for traditional weddings. Marriage is the expectation that the bride and groom will interconnect in such a way that they no longer have individually distinguishable traits. Genesis 2:24 states, "Therefore shall a man leave his father and his mother, and shall cleave unto his wife: and they shall be one joined flesh." The heavenly wedding will last forever.

No More Divorces

Mat. 19:9   And I say unto you, Whosoever shall put away his wife, except *it be* for fornication, and shall marry another, committeth adultery: and whoso marrieth her which is put away doth commit adultery.

Jesus, in His infinite knowledge, knew man would forsake the marriage covenant. He added a freedom clause to eliminate a person from being stuck in bondage when there are blatant acts against the marriage covenant. He allowed divorce only on the grounds of fornication (Mat. 19:9). In marriage, the two individuals are bound to remain married to each other, except in the case of sexual immorality. This act excludes the devoted spouse from bondage. The faithful husband or wife is still pure and not obligated to become tainted with the stain of a third party introduced into the marriage by the unfaithful spouse. The unreliable party has joined or became one flesh with another. Sexual immorality is an abomination to God. Jesus made it very clear, marriage is forever. There is only one reason for divorce, and that's fornication.

By today's standards, the accepted definition of fornication is sexual intercourse between single individuals, and adultery is sexual intercourse outside of marriage. According to these definitions, fornication and adultery is sexual intercourse with anyone other than a spouse. A closer examination of the word fornication shows that it is *any form* of sexual misconduct. Fornication is inclusive of adultery, homosexuality, incest, pornography, etc. Adultery is limited to sexual intercourse with someone other than a spouse. Fornication is sexual misconduct with a person, place, or thing, and it also includes the use of the sexual organs outside of their intended purpose. Adultery is to fornication, as embezzlement is to theft. Adultery falls under the category of fornication. Divorce can only be valid if the reason is sexual immorality (fornication). Note, in a heavenly wedding, there is no divorce because there is no unfaithfulness.

The Living Quarters

Joh. 14:2   In my Father's house are many mansions: if *it were* not *so*, I would have told you. I go to prepare a place for you.

Joh. 14:3   And if I go and prepare a place for you, I will come again, and receive you unto myself; that where I am, *there* ye may be also.

In any royal wedding, the bride and groom receive living quarters. After a bride is engaged, it's customary for the groom to prepare a home for them, and the bride waits patiently for the groom's return. This same custom applies to a heavenly wedding. Jesus is the groom, and He also went away to prepare for the marriage. Jesus ascended to heaven to prepare a place for His bride. When He returns, it will be time for the wedding. Jesus is in heaven now, making all of the necessary arrangements in preparation to receive His bride. There are many mansions in His Father's house. Once His home is complete, He will return for His bride, and the wedding will begin.

Rev. 3:12   Him that overcometh will I make a pillar in the temple of my God, and he shall go no more out: and I will write upon him the name of my God, and the name of the city of my God, *which is* new Jerusalem, which cometh down out of heaven from my God: and *I will write upon him* my new name.

In the heavenly wedding, the bride will become a pillar of support in her new home. Usually, the bride takes on the last name of the groom. In the heavenly wedding, the name changes are more significant. The celestial marriage takes the name change to a whole new level. The name change is three-fold. It consists of a new name, God's name, and the city of God. A heavenly wedding not only changes the bride's name, but it is also an identity change, where the bride becomes a part of the spiritual royal family.

The Marriage Benefits

1Pe. 2:9   But ye *are* a chosen generation, a royal priesthood, an holy nation, a peculiar people; that ye should shew forth the praises of him who hath called you out of darkness into his marvellous light:

Rev. 1:6   And hath made us kings and priests unto God and his Father; to him *be* glory and dominion for ever and ever. Amen.

In a heavenly wedding, the bride is no longer subject to the restrictions adopted by the world. She's called out from the darkness of this world and will join the ranks of a chosen generation. The bride experiences perfect love, joy, peace, and happiness. She will become royalty in an instant. She will transition into a ruler and no longer one of the ruled.

As a part of the royal family, she's filled with that marvelous light that radiates from God the Father. She will have dominion over the entire earth, and her light of righteousness will shine into all the hidden and forbidden crevices of this world. No longer will the world be drab and iniquitous, but the light of truth and justice will shine throughout the world.

1Jo. 3:2   Beloved, now are we the sons of God, and it doth not yet appear what we shall be: but we know that, when he shall appear, we shall be like him; for we shall see him as he is.

Php. 3:21   Who shall change our vile body, that it may be fashioned like unto his glorious body, according to the working whereby he is able even to subdue all things unto himself.

In traditional weddings, neither the bride nor the groom experience any physical changes. In a heavenly marriage, the bride will undergo a total and complete makeover. Automatically, she will inherit a brand-new body to replace the old one. The new body will be identical to the one Jesus possessed after His resurrection, but without the nail holes. This new body is immortal and often referenced as a glorified body. It will be immune to sickness, disease, aches, and pains. The need to regularly visit members of the medical profession and consume medications will be a thing of the past. Life will be outstanding, and the aging process will be non-existent.

The Bride's New Diet

Rev. 2:7   He that hath an ear, let him hear what the Spirit saith unto the churches; To him that overcometh will I give to eat of the tree of life, which is in the midst of the paradise of God.

Rev. 2:17   He that hath an ear, let him hear what the Spirit saith unto the churches; To him that overcometh will I give to eat of the hidden manna, and will give him a white stone, and in the stone a new name written, which no man knoweth saving he that receiveth it.

At the Lamb's marriage, the bride will have the right and authority to partake of the fruit from the Tree of Life. The fruit of the Tree of Life is the same fruit that Adam and Eve ate before their fall in the Garden of Eden. While they ate of this fruit, they were empowered to live forever because the fruit of the Tree of Life provisions the energy to keep the body fully charged. Likewise, any mortals that eat fruit from the Tree of Life will live until he stops eating the fruit. Genesis 3:22 states, "The man is become as one of us, to know good and evil: and now, lest he put forth his

hand, and take also of the Tree of Life, and eat, and live for ever."
After Adam and Eve's fall, God placed cherubim at the Tree of
Life to prevent them from eating from it anymore. Genesis 3:24
states, "He drove out the man; and he placed at the east of the
garden of Eden Cherubims, and a flaming sword which turned
every way, to keep the way of the tree of life."

Not only will the bride be granted permission to partake of
the Tree of Life, but she will also be allowed to eat manna.
Revelation 2:17 states, "To him that overcometh will I give to eat
of the hidden manna." Manna is the same bread that the Children
of Israel ate while wandering in the wilderness for forty years.
During that time, there were no sicknesses or diseases because
manna has supernatural healing powers. Manna also has the
classification of angels' food (Psa. 78:24-25). After the
resurrection, the resurrected saints' body is synonymous to angel's
bodies; therefore, it's permissible for them to partake of the manna
that's presently hidden from man.

The Bride's Medical Coverage

> Rev. 21:4   And God shall wipe away all tears from their eyes;
> and there shall be no more death, neither sorrow,
> nor crying, neither shall there be any more pain:
> for the former things are passed away.

When a spouse marries into a royal family, he or she instantly
becomes covered by the best medical coverage the government has
to offer. The medical coverage has no policy because medical
treatment isn't applicable in heaven. There's no sickness and
disease in the celestial kingdom; therefore, medical coverage is not
an option. It just isn't offered because there will be no medical
needs or emergencies. Even if it is possible to lose a limb from an
accident, the victim will instantaneously grow another limb to
replace it. There isn't any need for any medical insurance in the
heavenly kingdom because the saints have the *assurance* that God
will supply all their needs.

The Bride's Transportation

Rev. 19:11   And I saw heaven opened, and behold a white horse; and he that sat upon him *was* called Faithful and True, and in righteousness he doth judge and make war.

Rev. 19:12   His eyes *were* as a flame of fire, and on his head *were* many crowns; and he had a name written, that no man knew, but he himself.

Rev. 19:13   And he *was* clothed with a vesture dipped in blood: and his name is called The Word of God.

Rev. 19:14   And the armies *which were* in heaven followed him upon white horses, clothed in fine linen, white and clean.

In a traditional royal wedding, the spouse marrying into the royal family, transportation needs are upgraded. They have access to the best planes, boats, cars, etc. Their improved transportation is vastly improved compared to their travel arrangements before the royal wedding. At first glance, it appears that the traditional royal wedding's transportation services are far superior to transportation in a heavenly marriage. The method of transportation in a celestial wedding seems to be limited to horseback riding. Please be mindful, the horse is a white horse that travels at the speed of light, and the horse is riding on a cloud, powered by the Holy Spirit.

1Th. 4:17   Then we which are alive *and* remain shall be caught up together with them in the clouds, to meet the Lord in the air: and so shall we ever be with the Lord.

Although horseback riding is usually slower than boats, cars, and planes, the horses in the heavenly kingdom have an added advantage. They will be traveling on clouds that move through the atmosphere with no wind resistance. Neither does these horses or clouds require any organic nor petroleum fuels. The wind usually powers clouds. In Hebrew, the Strong's number for the word *wind* is #H7307. The definition of *wind* and *spirit* is identical; therefore, the clouds transport the horses, and the Holy Spirit powers the clouds.

Selection of the Wedding Date?

Mat. 24:36   But of that day and hour knoweth no *man*, no, not the angels of heaven, but my Father only.

Usually, the wedding date is decided upon by the bride and groom, but in the heavenly marriage, this isn't the case. Neither the bride nor the groom will have a say in determining the wedding date. That honor belongs to the father of the groom. No one on earth or in heaven except God the Father knows the date or the heavenly wedding's timing. There are many false predictions, but the actual date of the wedding remains classified.

When is the Heavenly Wedding?

Mat. 24:5   For many shall come in my name, saying, I am Christ; and shall deceive many.

Mat. 24:6   And ye shall hear of wars and rumours of wars: see that ye be not troubled: for all *these things* must come to pass, but the end is not yet.

Mat. 24:7   For nation shall rise against nation, and kingdom against kingdom: and there shall be famines, and pestilences, and earthquakes, in divers places.

Mat. 24:8   All these *are* the beginning of sorrows.

Although no one knows the heavenly wedding's actual date, scripture provides clues about the wedding's season. The fulfillment of Bible prophecy in conjunction with current events is how we can discern the wedding season's closeness. Just as one knows summer is near when the flowers began to bloom, we can also determine that the royal wedding is close when we see one nation rise against another nation and one kingdom rise against another kingdom. These uprisings, coupled with famines, pestilences, and earthquakes occurring worldwide, signify that the heavenly wedding is near.

All Bible prophecy centers around the nation of Israel. One significant indication that the heavenly wedding is near is that Israel became a state in 1948, and today, Israel's enemies almost surround her. In the years 2011 and 2012, there were numerous conflicts and uprisings in the Middle-east. Something else to observe with extraordinary curiosity is the world's bombardment with tornados, earthquakes, and tsunamis. Some of the world's pestilences are cancer, aids, bird flu, Ebola, Corona Virus, and flesh-eating bacteria. These things, coupled with famine throughout the world, are an excellent indication that we are in the season for the heavenly wedding.

The Heavenly Wedding's Venue

Zec. 14:4   And his feet shall stand in that day upon the mount of Olives, which *is* before Jerusalem on the east, and the mount of Olives shall cleave in the midst thereof toward the east and toward the west, *and there shall be* a very great valley; and half of the mountain shall remove toward the north, and half of it toward the south.

Zec. 14:5   And ye shall flee *to* the valley of the mountains; for the valley of the mountains shall reach unto Azal: yea, ye shall flee, like as ye fled from before the earthquake in the days of Uzziah king of Judah: and the LORD my God shall come, *and* all the saints with thee.

Zec. 14:6   And it shall come to pass in that day, *that* the light shall not be clear, *nor* dark:

Zec. 14:7   But it shall be one day which shall be known to the LORD, not day, nor night: but it shall come to pass, *that* at evening time it shall be light.

Zec. 14:8   And it shall be in that day, *that* living waters shall go out from Jerusalem; half of them toward the former sea, and half of them toward the hinder sea: in summer and in winter shall it be.

> Zec. 14:9   And the LORD shall be king over all the earth: in
>   that day shall there be one LORD, and his name
>   one.

All weddings are pre-planned, right down to the physical location of the festivities. The invitations are printed and mailed to all the guests to provide them with all the pertinent details. The Marriage of the Lamb is no different because everyone receives a written invitation—the Bible. It records the location of the ceremony. Some might think the royal wedding will be in the air (sky) when the saints meet the Lord. Scripture is quite clear that the Marriage of the Lamb will take place in Jerusalem. The invitation is so complete that it almost included the GPS coordinates. The location is in a suburb, east of the City of Jerusalem, on the Mount of Olives.

> Mic. 4:7   And I will make her that halted a remnant, and
>   her that was cast far off a strong nation: and the
>   LORD shall reign over them in mount Zion from
>   henceforth, even for ever.

Mount Zion is another name that comes to mind when speaking of the Marriage of the Lamb. Mount Zion is also called Jerusalem or the City of David. Jerusalem is the city in which Jesus will establish His kingdom and rule forever. Regardless of the name used, whether it is Mount Zion, Mount of Olives, City of David, or Jerusalem, the location and proximities are synonymous.

The Bride and Groom's Kingdom

> Rev. 5:10   And hast made us unto our God kings and
>   priests: and we shall reign on the earth.

All too often, people make mention that the bride will live in heaven. To most people, heaven is up in the sky, somewhere beyond the clouds. Heaven is wherever God is, at any given moment. It's not necessarily in outer space somewhere. Scripture confirms that God will dwell on earth with His bride. Revelation 21:3 states, "The tabernacle of God is with men, and he will dwell with them" As the bride resides in New Jerusalem with Jesus, she will also rule and reign with Him. Revelation 20:6 states, "But they shall be priests of God and of Christ, and shall reign with him a thousand years." During the thousand-year reign, the bride will co-rule over the nations. The nations are not in heaven; they are right here on earth. Scripture supports all of this information. Armed with these facts, it is conceivable to conclude that the bride and groom's kingdom is right here on earth.

The Bride and Groom's Subjects

Mat. 24:40   Then shall two be in the field; the one shall be taken, and the other left.

Mat. 24:41   Two *women shall be* grinding at the mill; the one shall be taken, and the other left.

In any kingdom, the people are under the authority of the government. More often than not, the government classifies its inhabitants as citizens, but their classification is *subjects* in a traditional kingdom. The *subjects* in Jesus' everlasting kingdom are not the saints, but those *left behind*. In Jesus' eternal kingdom, the saints are not the ones reigned over, but they are the ones that are reigning. Revelation 2:26-27 states, "He that overcometh, and keepeth my works unto the end, to him will I give power over the nations ... he shall rule them with a rod of iron." The left-behind individuals are the subjects, better known as the nations. The bride and groom will reign over them with the Word of God.

The Groom in the Heavenly Wedding

In every wedding, there must be a groom; the heavenly marriage is no different. The groom in this wedding is the Lamb. The question becomes, who is the Lamb? The answer is, Jesus is the Lamb. John 1:36 states, "Looking upon Jesus as he walked, he saith, Behold the Lamb of God!"

Accepting the idea that the Lamb is the groom might seem a little odd, but in the Old Testament, they sacrifice a lamb as the sacrificial lamb for the people's sins. The same precept continued into the New Testament when Jesus died on the cross as a sacrificial offering for the sins of the world. John 1:29 states, "John seeth Jesus coming unto him, and saith, Behold the Lamb of God, which taketh away the sin of the world."

Jesus is the Lamb of God. Not only is He the Lamb of God; more importantly, He is also the Son of God. Because He is the Son of God, that also makes Him the heir. Hebrews 1:2 states, "In these last days spoken unto us by his Son, whom he hath appointed heir of all things." Just as all kings want their sons to get married, God is no different. He has planned a massive wedding for His Son. Jesus Christ is God's only begotten son; therefore, Jesus is the groom in the heavenly marriage.

Christ's Relationship with the Church

> Mat. 16:18   And I say also unto thee, That thou art Peter, and upon this rock I will build my church; and the gates of hell shall not prevail against it.

Jesus Christ is the groom in the heavenly wedding, so what is His relationship with the church? First of all, what is the church? The first time someone mentions *the church* in scripture (KJV) is in Matthew 16:18, and it references Jesus telling Peter that He will build His church upon a rock. Although Peter's name means rock or stone, he was not the rock that Jesus stated He would construct His church. Jesus Christ, who is also known as *The Word*, is that rock. Yes, Jesus charged Peter with building a church, with a stone as its foundation, but the foundation was not Peter; it was the Word of God. The church that Jesus appointed Peter to construct was not an actual church building; it was the people that congregate together that constitutes the church. The literal meaning of the word church is *a calling out or assembly of people.*

Eph. 5:23   For the husband is the head of the wife, even as Christ is the head of the church: and he is the saviour of the body.

Just as any successful organization has a leader or chief executive officer, the church is no different. The head of the church is Christ, simply because of what He did at Calvary. When He died on that cross, He became the savior of a body of believers, better known as the church. This body of believers is the same church that Peter, along with the other disciples, pioneered after Christ's death. The church or body of believers is known as the Body of Christ.

Col. 1:18   And he is the head of the body, the church: who is the beginning, the firstborn from the dead; that in all *things* he might have the preeminence.

Christ is the head of the church (Body of Christ). He was the first to die and resurrected from the dead with a glorified body; therefore, He is the preeminence or the head. Everyone who believes in Him will likewise follow this distinction of being raised from the dead. Because Christ's resurrection was the first with a new body, He is the head. Those raised from the dead after Jesus are called the Body of Christ. Jesus Christ is the head of the church, and the church is the Body of Christ.

The Body of Christ

1Co. 12:12   For as the body is one, and hath many members, and all the members of that one body, being many, are one body: so also *is* Christ.

The Body of Christ is a body of religious believers that are woven and knitted together with one common bond, Christ Jesus. He is the common denominator that is prominent in every Christian's life. The Church or Body of Christ is a coalition of repented individuals that have joined together to form one unit or body that is more dominant than individuals laboring alone. There is power in numbers. This union is similar to a marriage where two people join together to become one. Once a person has obtained salvation, he's automatically become a member of the Body of Christ. There aren't any other requirements or actions on their part, except for remaining faithful.

Every member of the Body of Christ is as equally important as the next member, no matter how insignificant their duties may seem. The pastor has no more importance than the custodian. Every individual performing his tasks with respect and dignity results in a reciprocal effect, and each function operates with ease and maximum return.

Do you recall the phrase, *too many chiefs*.? Well, in the Body of Christ, there are no chiefs.; everybody is equal. Every individual or member of the Body of Christ is precisely connected so that the body will perform like a well-oiled machine, where each member is dependent upon the other.

Sometimes individuals use the word *saints* when referencing the Body of Christ. There is nothing wrong with that phrasing. It's just another way of expressing the same thing. It doesn't matter which word or phrase you choose. They are all synonymous, whether they are called the saints, the church, or the Body of Christ.

The Demographics of the Church

When some say Christ will return to gather His church, they are purposely not including the Jewish people. They are insinuating the Jewish people aren't members of the Body of Christ. Another name for this doctrine is *replacement theology*. That could not be farther from the truth. When the Jews failed to recognize Jesus as the Messiah, He extended the covenant to the Gentiles. Jesus grafted the Gentiles into the branch that sustains the chosen people (Rom. 11:17). The church consists of Jews and Gentiles alike, and the common denominator is to be born-again.

Gal. 3:28   There is neither Jew nor Greek, there is neither bond nor free, there is neither male nor female: for ye are all one in Christ Jesus.

Gal. 3:29   And if ye *be* Christ's, then are ye Abraham's seed, and heirs according to the promise.

In Christ Jesus, we are all one if we believe in Jesus' death, burial, resurrection, and ascension into heaven. Every born-again individual, whether Jew or Gentile, belongs to the Body of Christ, which is also the church.

Everyone that is born-again of the spirit is a son of God. If you are a son of God, then you are also an heir. An heir is inclusive of every individual, regardless of his or her natural origin. The church is *any and every one* that's born-again when Christ returns to establish His everlasting kingdom, no matter their heritage.

Identifying the Bride of Christ

Rev. 21:9   And there came unto me one of the seven angels which had the seven vials full of the seven last plagues, and talked with me, saying, Come hither, I will shew thee the bride, the Lamb's wife.

Rev. 21:10   And he carried me away in the spirit to a great and high mountain, and shewed me that great city, the holy Jerusalem, descending out of heaven from God,

So many Christians think the Bride of Christ is the Church. Unfortunately, this viewpoint is in error. Scripture is unequivocal concerning the identity of the Bride of Christ. Revelation 21:1-4 paints us a picture of a city descending from heaven prepared as a bride. One of the angels in Revelation 21:9-10 goes even further and reveals the Bride of Christ's identity. The Holy City, New Jerusalem, descending from heaven is the Bride of Christ. Perhaps this doesn't sit well with many believers, but this is what scripture states.

The church is not the Bride of Christ. The church is the Body of Christ. Jesus is the head, and the church is the body. The *head* plus the *body* makes one complete entity. Every individual has a head and a body. The Body of Christ (church) connected to the head (Jesus) makes one whole being. Hebrews 4:14, states, "Seeing then … Jesus is the Son of God." According to Hebrews 1:2, Jesus, the Son is the heir of all things. Every born-again individual receives a sons' adoption; thereby, he is an heir (Gal. 4:4-7). Because born-again individuals (Body of Christ) are the children of God, they are joint-heirs with Christ (Rom. 8:14-17). Jesus is the head of the church (Body of Christ), and He is the heir. The Body of Christ becomes one with Jesus. The union of Jesus and the Body of Christ as one; make the Body of Christ a joint-heir.

There is something else to consider. If the head (Jesus) and the church (Body of Christ) are joint-heirs, then it is conceivable to believe that when Christ (head) returns for the church (Body of Christ), this union joins the head and the body together to complete only one being. This entity (Christ and Body of Christ) is the groom for the heavenly wedding. The groom (Christ plus the church) then enters the City (Bride of Christ) to dwell there, and this entrance is the marriage's consummation. The church is not the Bride of Christ; the church is the Body of Christ. The Bride of Christ is the holy city, New Jerusalem. Revelation 21:9-10 states, "Come hither, I will shew thee the bride, the Lamb's wife… and shewed me that great city, the holy Jerusalem, descending out of heaven from God." The church is the Body of Christ, and it is a joint-heir with Christ. Christ and the Body of Christ dwell as one unit, in the Bride of Christ, the Holy City, New Jerusalem.

Isa. 62:1   For Zion's sake will I not hold my peace, and for Jerusalem's sake I will not rest, until the righteousness thereof go forth as brightness, and the salvation thereof as a lamp *that* burneth.

Isa. 62:2   And the Gentiles shall see thy righteousness, and all kings thy glory: and thou shalt be called by a new name, which the mouth of the LORD shall name.

Isa. 62:3	Thou shalt also be a crown of glory in the hand of the LORD, and a royal diadem in the hand of thy God.
Isa. 62:4	Thou shalt no more be termed Forsaken; neither shall thy land any more be termed Desolate: but thou shalt be called Hephzibah, and thy land Beulah: for the LORD delighteth in thee, and thy land shall be married.
Isa. 62:5	For *as* a young man marrieth a virgin, *so* shall thy sons marry thee: and *as* the bridegroom rejoiceth over the bride, *so* shall thy God rejoice over thee.

The Marriage of the Lamb is when the Body of Christ is resurrected and given new names. They will then become royalty and declared to be kings and priests. They will rule and reign with Christ. The marriage is not the Lamb joining with the Body of Christ. The marriage is the Lamb and the Body of Christ joining to the land. That land or real estate is the Holy City, New Jerusalem. The Holy City is the place Christ was referencing when He stated He would prepare a home for the Body of Christ.

| Joh. 14:2 | In my Father's house are many mansions: if *it were* not *so*, I would have told you. I go to prepare a place for you. |
| Joh. 14:3 | And if I go and prepare a place for you, I will come again, and receive you unto myself; that where I am, *there* ye may be also. |

Jesus went to heaven to prepare a place for His body to live. Jesus, the head, already has a glorified body and has access to heaven. At this moment, the Body of Christ does not have access to heaven, merely because they have not yet received a glorified body. Once the Body of Christ gets its glorified body, it will be joined or connected to the head (Jesus). It will not be married to the head (Jesus), but it will become a part of Jesus, forming one complete entity. Once the head and body join together, the two will become one. This union establishes the groom. Consummation occurs when the groom (head and body) enters into New Jerusalem, which is the Bride of Christ, the Lamb's wife.

CHAPTER 12

THE MILLENNIUM

WHEN discussing the events of the End-times, the word *Millennium* always surfaces. In the KJV of the Bible, the word Millennium is not in the text, but scripture refers to it throughout the book of Revelation. Millennium means a period that spans one thousand years. Just as ten years equal a decade and one hundred years equal a century, one thousand years is equivalent to a Millennium. This chapter focuses entirely on the Millennium or first one thousand years after the return of Christ. The following are some examples of how the Bible references the millennial period.

Rev. 20:4   And I saw thrones, and they sat upon them, and judgment was given unto them: and I saw the souls of them that were beheaded for the witness of Jesus, and for the word of God, and which had not worshipped the beast, neither his image, neither had received his mark upon their foreheads, or in their hands; and they lived and reigned with Christ a thousand years.

Rev. 20:6   Blessed and holy is he that hath part in the first resurrection: on such the second death hath no power, but they shall be priests of God and of Christ, and shall reign with him a thousand years.

Many people acknowledge the thousand-year reign as the Millennial kingdom. We know the Millennium is 1000 years after the return of Christ, so let's look at the definition of *kingdom* to grasp a better understanding of the phrase Millennial kingdom. The word *kingdom* means the domain in which something is dominant, an environment, or a walk of life. Kings, queens, dictators, etc. have authority and reign over territories. Usually, a domain is a country or nation. An example of a present-day kingdom is the country of England. Kingdoms don't have a president or emperor; they have a king or queen.

The Millennial kingdom is the territory that God will reign over when He establishes His everlasting kingdom. That kingdom will be here on earth, and the time frame of the Millennial kingdom is between the Second Coming (First Resurrection) and the Little Season (Rev. 20:3). The notion that a Millennial kingdom is a physical place or a spiritual place differs according to one's understanding of the scriptures. To the resurrected saints, the Millennium is a spiritual awareness because their old bodies transform into a spiritual body. Concerning the sheep nations, the Millennium is a physical awareness because they reside here on earth but are still subject to the laws of life and death.

The Millennial Kingdom's Inhabitants

Mat. 24:40   Then shall two be in the field; the one shall be taken, and the other left.

Mat. 24:41   Two women shall be grinding at the mill; the one shall be taken, and the other left.

The Millennium kingdom will consist of two groups of people or entities. The two groups are immortals and mortals. The immortals are the individuals that were born-again at the First Resurrection or return of Christ. At His return, the fleshly bodies of righteous individuals transform into a new spiritual body. These are the saints, and they are classified as the ones-taken (raptured) when Christ returns. The saint's physical body changing into a spiritual body parallels with scripture. Philippians 3:21 states, "Who shall change our vile body, that it may be fashioned like unto his glorious body." The saint's new body will be similar to the resurrected body of Christ. 1 Corinthians 15:54 states, "When this corruptible shall have put on incorruption, and this mortal shall have put on immortality, then shall be brought to pass the saying that is written, Death is swallowed up in victory." The resurrected saints are spiritual or immortal body recipients, but they reign in a physical world.

The mortals are those individuals or nations that are left-behind when Christ returns for His saints. They are called the sheep nations, and they will inherit the Millennial kingdom, but they will not inherit a spiritual body. They will be subject to the authority of the ones-taken (saints) who received their immortal bodies at the return of Christ.

The Living Conditions of the Saints

Rev. 7:9   After this I beheld, and, lo, a great multitude, which no man could number, of all nations, and kindreds, and people, and tongues, stood before the throne, and before the Lamb, clothed with white robes, and palms in their hands;

Rev. 7:10   And cried with a loud voice, saying, Salvation to our God which sitteth upon the throne, and unto the Lamb.

Rev. 7:11   And all the angels stood round about the throne, and about the elders and the four beasts, and fell before the throne on their faces, and worshipped God,

Rev. 7:12   Saying, Amen: Blessing, and glory, and wisdom, and thanksgiving, and honour, and power, and might, be unto our God for ever and ever. Amen.

Rev. 7:13   And one of the elders answered, saying unto me, What are these which are arrayed in white robes? and whence came they?

Rev. 7:14   And I said unto him, Sir, thou knowest. And he said to me, These are they which came out of great tribulation, and have washed their robes, and made them white in the blood of the Lamb.

Rev. 7:15   Therefore are they before the throne of God, and serve him day and night in his temple: and he that sitteth on the throne shall dwell among them.

Rev. 7:16   They shall hunger no more, neither thirst any more; neither shall the sun light on them, nor any heat.

Rev. 7:17   For the Lamb which is in the midst of the throne shall feed them, and shall lead them unto living fountains of waters: and God shall wipe away all tears from their eyes.

There's a vast multitude of individuals gathered from all around the world. They are standing before the throne of God, dressed in white. They are blessing and praising Almighty God. These are the saints that received a new body when Christ returned. They are in the presence of God, where they dwell and serve Him day and night. They receive their orientation to prepare to live in a perfect environment, the Millennial kingdom.

The mortals, on the other hand, are the ones left- behind. The Lord divides them into two groups, known as the sheep nations and the goat nations. Both of these remnants face judgment. The Lord sentence the goats to Hell and He sentence the sheep to reside in the Millennial kingdom. The sheep will not receive a new body, merely because they were not born-again at the return of Christ. Both the sheep and the goats are un-repented, and that's the reason they are left behind. The sheep and goats' difference is the goat openly denounced the Holy Spirit, and the sheep did not. Openly criticizing the Holy Spirit is committing the Unpardonable Sin, which is the only sin that the Lord will not grant forgiveness. Blasphemy of the Holy Ghost is the Unpardonable Sin, and it is the deciding factor that segregates the sheep that live in the Millennial kingdom from the goats that live in Hell-fire. The sheep will live in the Millennial kingdom, but their fleshly bodies are not changed; therefore, they remain mortals.

The Immortal Body

Joh. 20:19   Then the same day at evening, being the first day of the week, when the doors were shut where the disciples were assembled for fear of the Jews, came Jesus and stood in the midst, and saith unto them, Peace be unto you.

Joh. 20:27   Then saith he to Thomas, Reach hither thy finger, and behold my hands; and reach hither thy hand, and thrust it into my side: and be not faithless, but believing.

Luk. 24:39   Behold my hands and my feet, that it is I myself: handle me, and see; for a spirit hath not flesh and bones, as ye see me have.

1Co. 15:50   Now this I say, brethren, that flesh and blood cannot inherit the kingdom of God; neither doth corruption inherit incorruption.

The saint's earthly body transforms into a new body at the First Resurrection. Their new body will be comparable to Jesus' resurrected body, minus the nail holes. The saint's new body can be physically handled and respond to touch. It will have flesh and bone, but it will not have any blood. The saints' glorified body will be versatile; therefore, it can respond as a physical body and as a spiritual body. When they act in a spiritual state, their bodies can penetrate walls and even be invisible at times. Jesus demonstrated this when He entered the room where His disciples were gathered while the door was still closed.

The Duties of the Saints

Rev. 7:9   After this I beheld, and, lo, a great multitude, which no man could number, of all nations, and kindreds, and people, and tongues, stood before the throne, and before the Lamb, clothed with white robes, and palms in their hands;

Rev. 7:10   And cried with a loud voice, saying, Salvation to our God which sitteth upon the throne, and unto the Lamb.

Let's take a look at some of the saints' duties once they take up residence in the Millennial kingdom. The first official act and most distinguished privilege are to immerse themselves in praising Almighty God. They are no longer just ordinary citizens of a country, but they are dignitaries of an everlasting kingdom and honored with titles of royalty. Revelation 1:6 states, "And hath made us kings and priests unto God and his Father; to him be glory and dominion for ever and ever." Once the Lord crown the saints as kings and priests, they receive their rewards and assume their first term in office, which is one thousand years. Revelation 20:4 states, "And they lived and reigned with Christ a thousand years."

Every king and priest must have a kingdom and (or) congregation of subjects to govern. The saints receive authority over the nations. Revelation 2:26-27 states, "He that overcometh, and keepeth my works unto the end, to him will I give power over the nations … he shall rule them with a rod of iron." The nations will be the individuals that are left behind. Remember, those left-behind will be divided into two groups, resulting in the goats going into Hell-fire and the sheep remaining on earth. The sheep will be the only mortals left on earth, and they will be the nations that the saints rule with a rod of iron.

The sheep nations will be allowed to live in the Millennial kingdom. Because they are left behind, they will remain here on earth. Note, the sheep will have access to the entire world, except New Jerusalem. Only the saints, who reign over the sheep, will have access to New Jerusalem. Revelation 5:10 states, "And hast made us unto our God kings and priests: and we shall reign on the earth." Because the sheep nations are residing on earth, and the saints are ruling over them on earth, the Millennial kingdom's domain is on planet earth.

Not only are the saints going to reign over the sheep who are left behind, but they will also have other duties. Because the saints are immortal, they will also have to act as judge and jury over earthly and heavenly beings. 1 Corinthians 6:3 states, "Know ye not that we shall judge angels?"

The Saints and Matrimony

Mat. 22:30   For in the resurrection they neither marry, nor are given in marriage, but are as the angels of God in heaven.

In the Millennial kingdom, the saints will not be married to their same earthly spouses whom they previously married. They will no longer be a married couple. In the resurrection, the saints are exactly like the angels, who do not have spouses. Yes, husbands and wives will know each other and love each other, but it's not that kind of love. There will be no cohabitation and no sexual intimacy. If earthly marriages of saints resumed into the Millennium, it would present an awkward situation, mostly when there were multiple marriages by either the husband and the wife. The love shared by the saints in heaven or the Millennial kingdom is equivalent to the love that a mother has for a child.

In the Millennial kingdom, the saint's biological children will not be considered their offspring. Parents will know their children, and the children will know their parents, but there will not be individual families. All of the saints will be members of the same family, the Body of Christ.

In the case of the sheep nations, everything will continue as it did before the return of Christ. They will continue to marry, bear children, work, etc. The only significant difference is that they are now under the authority of the saints. Some sheep fall under the jurisdiction of the saints whom they mistreated in the Pre-Millennium era, but there's no ill-will on behalf of the saints, because they are righteous.

The Saint's Dining Habits

Luk. 24:42   And they gave him a piece of a broiled fish, and of an honeycomb.
Luk. 24:43   And he took it, and did eat before them.

In the Millennial kingdom, the saints will have a new body equivalent to the resurrected body of Jesus. On Resurrection Day, Jesus visited His disciples, and He asked them for some food. They gave Him physical or ordinary food, and He did eat it. Perhaps Jesus ate regular food because He was still living here on earth, and He needed nutrition. He lived on earth for forty days before He ascended into heaven. The food provisioned to the saints in the Millennial kingdom comes directly from the Tree of Life, and they will drink Living Water. The fruit from the Tree of Life and the Living Water provides the saint's nourishment and eternal life. There is an added benefit of this food; it is both gluten-free and calorie-free.

> Rev. 2:7   He that hath an ear, let him hear what the Spirit saith unto the churches; To him that overcometh will I give to eat of the tree of life, which is in the midst of the paradise of God.

> Rev. 22:14 Blessed are they that do his commandments, that they may have right to the tree of life, and may enter in through the gates into the city.

In the Millennial kingdom, the saints will have access to the Tree of Life. It is the fruit of the Tree of Life that allows them to live forever. Upon Adam's expulsion from the Garden of Eden, God placed cherubim to prevent him from partaking from the Tree of Life again. Genesis 3:22 states, "The LORD God said, Behold, the man is become as one of us, to know good and evil: and now, lest he put forth his hand, and take also of the tree of life, and eat, and live for ever."

> Rev. 22:1   And he shewed me a pure river of water of life, clear as crystal, proceeding out of the throne of God and of the Lamb.

> Rev. 22:17 And the Spirit and the bride say, Come. And let him that heareth say, Come. And let him that is

athirst come. And whosoever will, let him take
the water of life freely.

Not only will the saints have unlimited access to the Tree of
Life, but they will also be permitted to drink from the pure water
of life. Perfect water that sustains life is Living Water. The water
that Jesus offered the woman at the well was Living Water. John
4:14 states, "Whosoever drinketh of the water that I shall give him
shall never thirst; but the water that I shall give him shall be in him
a well of water springing up into everlasting life."

The Sheep's Dining Habits

The sheep nations cannot eat from the Tree of Life. They will
not be worthy to receive a new body when Christ returns;
therefore, they remain in their mortal bodies. If they were allowed
to eat from the Tree of Life, they would live forever, just as the
saints.

The sheep nations use the leaves from the Tree of Life for
their healing. Because they are left-behind with mortal bodies, they
will still have the same sicknesses and diseases before Christ's
return. Their healing isn't instantaneous. Only the saints will be
healed at His return when their mortal are bodies transitioned into
spiritual bodies. The healing and recovery of the mortals that
entered the Millennium with sickness will progressively begin to
improve due to eating the leaves from the Tree of Life.

The healing power the sheep experience from consumption
of the leaves from the Tree of Life is comparable to the healing
properties of the manna the Children of Israel enjoyed in the
wilderness. While they ate the manna in the wilderness, they did
not get sick. In the Millennium, the medical profession's services
will diminish rapidly because the leaves from the Tree of Life will
aid the healing process. Sickness and disease are like a free radical.
If they refuse to consume the leaves from the Tree of Life, their
bodies will become a fertile breeding ground for all kinds of
illnesses.

The Sheep in the Millennium

> Rev. 22:14   Blessed are they that do his commandments, that they may have right to the tree of life, and may enter in through the gates into the city.
>
> Rev. 22:15   For without are dogs, and sorcerers, and whoremongers, and murderers, and idolaters, and whosoever loveth and maketh a lie.

Although the sheep nations will live in the Millennial kingdom, they will not be permitted to go inside New Jerusalem. Only the saints will be allowed to enter this city. At the resurrection, the sheep nations will be unrighteous and not worthy to receive new spiritual bodies; therefore, they must remain on the outside of the New Jerusalem, the Holy City.

> Zec. 14:16   And it shall come to pass, that every one that is left of all the nations which came against Jerusalem shall even go up from year to year to worship the King, the LORD of hosts, and to keep the feast of tabernacles.
>
> Zec. 14:17   And it shall be, that whoso will not come up of all the families of the earth unto Jerusalem to worship the King, the LORD of hosts, even upon them shall be no rain.

The sheep nations will have to travel to New Jerusalem annually to keep the Feast of Tabernacles. When they go to New Jerusalem, they will be allowed to enter the courtyard area, but not the city itself. Only the priests (saints) are permitted to enter the inner court. The Feast of Tabernacles' annual observance patterns itself after the tabernacle in the wilderness and the temple in Jerusalem. The Feast of Tabernacles was a meaningful ceremony and mandatory for all the males to attend the feast annually. In the Millennium, if the sheep nations failed to participate in this feast, they will experience the plagues of Egypt.

Joe. 2:32   And it shall come to pass, that whosoever shall
             call on the name of the LORD shall be delivered:
             for in mount Zion and in Jerusalem shall be
             deliverance, as the LORD hath said, and in the
             remnant whom the LORD shall call.

The sheep nations will be in an un-repented state at the time
of Christ's return. During the Millennial period, they will have the
opportunity to become born-again. At that time, those born-again
are not Tribulation-saints; they are Millennial-saints because the
Tribulation has already passed, and they reside in the Millennial
kingdom. Anyone who repents during the Millennial kingdom and
maintains their salvation receives a spiritual body at the Great
White Throne Judgment. On the other hand, anyone that repents
during the Millennium but turns away from following God's word
will experience Hell-fire.

General Conditions in the Millennium

Rev. 20:1   And I saw an angel come down from heaven,
             having the key of the bottomless pit and a great
             chain in his hand.
Rev. 20:2   And he laid hold on the dragon, that old serpent,
             which is the Devil, and Satan, and bound him a
             thousand years,
Rev. 20:3   And cast him into the bottomless pit, and shut
             him up, and set a seal upon him, that he should
             deceive the nations no more, till the thousand
             years should be fulfilled: and after that he must
             be loosed a little season.

During the entire Millennial kingdom, The Lord confines
Satan in the Bottomless Pit. He will not be allowed to deceive the
sheep nations during that time. It is a period of peace on the earth,
but bear in mind, the mortals or sheep nations brought their
previous fleshly desires and tendencies over into the Millennial
kingdom. They will have to unlearn their naturally ingrained
behaviors with the assistance of the resurrected saints.

Isa. 2:2   And it shall come to pass in the last days, that the mountain of the LORD'S house shall be established in the top of the mountains, and shall be exalted above the hills; and all nations shall flow unto it.

Isa. 2:3   And many people shall go and say, Come ye, and let us go up to the mountain of the LORD, to the house of the God of Jacob; and he will teach us of his ways, and we will walk in his paths: for out of Zion shall go forth the law, and the word of the LORD from Jerusalem.

Isa. 2:4   And he shall judge among the nations, and shall rebuke many people: and they shall beat their swords into plowshares, and their spears into pruninghooks: nation shall not lift up sword against nation, neither shall they learn war any more.

Isa. 2:5   O house of Jacob, come ye, and let us walk in the light of the LORD.

With Satan bound, there is no more deception on the earth. Many of the sheep nations will go up to New Jerusalem to learn the ways of the Lord. The saints teach them to destroy all of their weapons for war and make gardening tools out of them. Because the Millennial kingdom is deception-free, the sheep nations can freely receive the Word of God and quickly incorporate it into their daily lives. Since the sheep nations are re-tooling from war weapons to agricultural tools, the Millennial kingdom will not need any military establishments.

Spiritual Conditions in the Millennium

Joe. 2:28   And it shall come to pass afterward, that I will pour out my spirit upon all flesh; and your sons and your daughters shall prophesy, your old men

shall dream dreams, your young men shall see
visions:

Joe. 2:29   And also upon the servants and upon the
handmaids in those days will I pour out my spirit.

Many teach the Lord implemented Joel 2:28-29 in Acts 2:4
concerning the Baptism of the Holy Spirit. That's not entirely
correct. Yes, the Lord did administer the Baptism of the Holy
Spirit on the Day of Pentecost. No, Joel 2:28-29 was not
referencing that event. It referenced the outpouring of the Holy
Spirit during the Millennial kingdom. The reason being, everybody
did not speak in other tongues on the Day of Pentecost, but the
Lord will pour out His Spirit upon all flesh in the Millennial
kingdom.

The keyword in these scriptures is *afterwards*. Now we have to
determine, *after what?* The scriptures are referencing a time after the
Tribulation but during the Millennial kingdom. The scripture states
that sons and daughters will prophesy, older men will dream
dreams, and young men will see visions. These things will take
place during the Millennial kingdom, while Satan is bound for one
thousand years. In those days, God will pour out His spirit upon
all flesh.

Isa. 11:1   And there shall come forth a rod out of the stem
of Jesse, and a Branch shall grow out of his roots:

Isa. 11:2   And the spirit of the LORD shall rest upon him,
the spirit of wisdom and understanding, the spirit
of counsel and might, the spirit of knowledge and
of the fear of the LORD;

Isa. 11:3   And shall make him of quick understanding in the
fear of the LORD: and he shall not judge after
the sight of his eyes, neither reprove after the
hearing of his ears:

Isa. 11:4   But with righteousness shall he judge the poor,
and reprove with equity for the meek of the earth:
and he shall smite the earth with the rod of his
mouth, and with the breath of his lips shall he slay
the wicked.

Isa. 11:5   And righteousness shall be the girdle of his loins, and faithfulness the girdle of his reins.

Isa. 11:6   The wolf also shall dwell with the lamb, and the leopard shall lie down with the kid; and the calf and the young lion and the fatling together; and a little child shall lead them.

Isa. 11:7   And the cow and the bear shall feed; their young ones shall lie down together: and the lion shall eat straw like the ox.

Isa. 11:8   And the sucking child shall play on the hole of the asp, and the weaned child shall put his hand on the cockatrice' den.

Isa. 11:9   They shall not hurt nor destroy in all my holy mountain: for the earth shall be full of the knowledge of the LORD, as the waters cover the sea.

Isaiah 11:1-9 is a future prophecy. It will not come to fruition until after the return of Christ and the Millennial kingdom is established. Jesus Christ is that rod that will come out of Jesse. He will not judge by what He sees and hears, but He will judge by the righteousness supplied by the Spirit of God.

In His kingdom, only righteousness will reign. The Lord will not tolerate unrighteousness at all. Morality is the purpose of His kingdom, and faithfulness is the nutrition to fulfill His purpose.

In the Millennial kingdom, the fruit of the spirit becomes the way of life. Even the animals will modify their behavior. The wolf will dwell with the lamb, and the leopard will lie down with the kid. Little children will not fear or be harmed by a snake. Nothing can exist in the Millennial kingdom that can cause damage or destruction—the Lord fills the Millennial kingdom with Godly knowledge and righteousness.

Isa. 65:17   For, behold, I create new heavens and a new earth: and the former shall not be remembered, nor come into mind.

Isa. 65:18   But be ye glad and rejoice for ever in that which I create: for, behold, I create Jerusalem a rejoicing, and her people a joy.

Isa. 65:19   And I will rejoice in Jerusalem, and joy in my people: and the voice of weeping shall be no more heard in her, nor the voice of crying.

Isa. 65:20   There shall be no more thence an infant of days, nor an old man that hath not filled his days: for the child shall die an hundred years old; but the sinner being an hundred years old shall be accursed.

Isa. 65:21   And they shall build houses, and inhabit them; and they shall plant vineyards, and eat the fruit of them.

Isa. 65:22   They shall not build, and another inhabit; they shall not plant, and another eat: for as the days of a tree are the days of my people, and mine elect shall long enjoy the work of their hands.

Isa. 65:23   They shall not labour in vain, nor bring forth for trouble; for they are the seed of the blessed of the LORD, and their offspring with them.

Isa. 65:24   And it shall come to pass, that before they call, I will answer; and while they are yet speaking, I will hear.

Isa. 65:25   The wolf and the lamb shall feed together, and the lion shall eat straw like the bullock: and dust shall be the serpent's meat. They shall not hurt nor destroy in all my holy mountain, saith the LORD.

In the Millennial kingdom, there will be no more premature deaths. Just as trees enjoy longevity, man will also enjoy long lives. No longer will man build houses, businesses, or anything and have it confiscated by a technicality. Man will benefit from the fruits of his labor.

Because righteousness will reign in the Millennial kingdom, it will cause God to give people the desires of their hearts before they even request it. Jesus, the king, will supply all of their needs. The Millennial kingdom is truly heaven. It is the utopian state where everything is perfect in all social, economic, political, and moral aspects of life.

CHAPTER 13

POST-MILLENNIUM

THE timing of the Millennium is immediately after the Tribulation Period. After the Tribulation Period, the First Resurrection takes place. The phrase *First Resurrection* can be somewhat controversial. Some say the *Rapture* occurs, and the *Second Coming* will follow sometime later. Using the phrase *First Resurrection* will minimize the confusion because it incorporates both the Rapture and the Second Coming. The First Resurrection is the return of Christ, and it precedes Him establishing His everlasting kingdom. The phrase *First Resurrection* is also scriptural. Revelation 20:4-5 states, "Which had not worshipped the beast, neither his image, neither had received his mark upon their foreheads, or in their hands; and they lived and reigned with Christ a thousand years ... This is the first resurrection." Once the seven-year Tribulation Period expires, the First Resurrection will occur, and then the Millennium will commence.

What is Post-Millennium?

The Millennium is a period of one thousand years inaugurated with Satan's incarceration in the Bottomless Pit. The Bottomless Pit is equivalent to a maximum-security prison where there's no possibility of parole or early release due to good behavior. During the Millennium, The Lord blankets the earth with peace because Satan is stripped of his authority to deceive people. The Millennium is the first thousand years of eternity, and it also coincides with the same period when the saints are reigning on earth with Christ.

Immediately after the conclusion of the thousand-year Millennium, another period emerges. It's called a Little Season or the Post-Millennium. The end of the Millennium brings about quite a few changes. It is the conclusion of Satan's incarceration, and it also brings to a close the thousand-year reign of the saints. Post-Millennium is the emergence of a whole new set of events. During the Millennium, the saints were the governing officials that reigned with the authority of Almighty God. Once the saints' reign has reached its fruition, the earth's inhabitants (sheep nations) will no longer have any spiritual influence from the saints. Every individual is responsible for maintaining his or her salvation.

> Rev. 20:2   And he laid hold on the dragon, that old serpent, which is the Devil, and Satan, and bound him a thousand years,
>
> Rev. 20:3   And cast him into the bottomless pit, and shut him up, and set a seal upon him, that he should deceive the nations no more, till the thousand years should be fulfilled: and after that he must be loosed a little season.

The earth has just undergone one thousand years of peace while being ruled by the saints. The world was free from deception because of Satan's incarceration in the Bottomless Pit. Simultaneously, two things come to an end after the Millennium: the saints' reign and Satan's imprisonment in the Bottomless Pit.

The Little Season

After Satan's release from the Bottomless Pit, he will return to earth. Michael and his angels permanently expelled him from heaven a little more than a thousand years earlier. Revelation 12:7-8, states "There was war in heaven: Michael and his angels fought against the dragon; and the dragon fought and his angels... prevailed not; neither was their place found any more in heaven." Satan's release from the Bottomless Pit will last for a short time. Scripture does not record how long this period will last. Scripture describes it as a *Little Season* or short amount of time.

Because the saint's thousand-year reign has expired, the world now has no organized governing officials to demand that man behaves himself in a virtuous manner. Scripture does not record the daily activities of the saints during the Post-Millennium period. Perhaps the saints now spend all of their time praising and worshipping Almighty God. Once the saints finished their thousand-year reign, the earth's inhabitants (sheep nations) are free to exercise their free-will without any saints' supervision. To compound the problem, people no longer enjoy freedom from deception because Satan has served his sentence and has regained his freedom. If imprisonment did not rehabilitate him from his previous lifestyle, the world would again have to contend with his antics of persecution and deception.

> Rev. 20:7   And when the thousand years are expired, Satan shall be loosed out of his prison,
>
> Rev. 20:8   And shall go out to deceive the nations which are in the four quarters of the earth, Gog and Magog, to gather them together to battle: the number of whom *is* as the sand of the sea.

It is safe to say, Satan's stint in the Bottomless Pit for one thousand years did not rehabilitate him. Soon after his release, he returns to earth, and much to his surprise, he finds the entire world practicing righteousness. For this reason, he re-introduces deception back into the world. Now, his sole mission is to persuade the earth's inhabitants that they need salvation from their *righteousness.* To accomplish his task, he marketed himself as God and explained that the saints had been deceiving them with their religious ideology for the last thousand years. According to Satan, it was time for them to stop living a lifestyle of righteousness and begin to experience life and enjoy it more abundantly, by Satan's standards.

Satan goes out into the entire world with the intent of deceiving the people once again. He musters together a massive army; whose size is innumerable. His army consists of the people enjoying a lifestyle of righteousness for the past one thousand years. The name of this vast military campaign is called *Gog and*

Magog. Gog is a title for a leader that's anti-god. Magog is the followers of Gog.

Satan is a spiritual entity, but he needs a human being to operate on his behalf in the physical world. He will recruit a man that he will overshadow and manipulate into leading his military campaign against the house of God. This man is essentially going to be against God Almighty; therefore, he assumes the title of Gog. This man is equivalent to the second Antichrist. The first Antichrist is in the Lake of Fire; Revelation 19:20 states, "The beast was taken, and with him the false prophet ... both were cast alive into a lake of fire burning with brimstone." Magog is all of the individuals that enlist in Satan's massive army.

The earth's inhabitants previously enjoyed perfect peace and experienced no deception for one thousand years. Now they find themselves without any moral guidance and no positive role-model. They have no standardized form of government because the saint's reign recently expired. Satan set about to deceive them, and he quickly accomplished his objective because they never experienced any form of deception.

Gog and Magog will strategically encompass New Jerusalem, the Holy City. They intended to attack with stealth and surgical precision in their campaign to destroy the dwelling place of God and the saints. Just as they are about to attack, God's supernatural ability to acquire information will disclose their position and intentions. With this information, God launches a successful counter-attack. He propels a barrage of fire from heaven that devours Satan's entire army. Yes, Satan succeeded in deceiving the nations but failed to complete his mission.

Why did God permit Satan's release from the Bottomless Pit? Scripture does not say why God released him. God is not a respecter of persons; perhaps God had to allow all the individuals born in the Millennium, *a Little Season,* to exercise their *free-will.* Before the point that Satan is released, they had never experienced any form of deception.

The people (sheep nations) who entered the Millennium from its beginning had experienced both deception and peace. They contended with Satan's evil power during the Tribulation Period, and they enjoyed a world of peace after Satan's confinement in the Bottomless Pit. Many of the individuals born during the Millennial period only knew a world without Satan's evil influences and never experienced temptation. They never experienced *choice or free-will.*

Joe. 2:28   And it shall come to pass afterward, *that* I will pour out my spirit upon all flesh; and your sons and your daughters shall prophesy, your old men shall dream dreams, your young men shall see visions:

Joe. 2:29   And also upon the servants and upon the handmaids in those days will I pour out my spirit.

Joe. 2:30   And I will shew wonders in the heavens and in the earth, blood, and fire, and pillars of smoke.

Joe. 2:31   The sun shall be turned into darkness, and the moon into blood, before the great and the terrible day of the LORD come.

Joe. 2:32   And it shall come to pass, *that* whosoever shall call on the name of the LORD shall be delivered: for in mount Zion and in Jerusalem shall be deliverance, as the LORD hath said, and in the remnant whom the LORD shall call.

Those individuals that are born in the Millennium received exposure to righteousness for their entire lives. The saints were reigning and teaching them the ways of the Lord. During the Millennium, the Lord will pour out His Spirit upon all flesh, humans, and animals alike (Isa. 11:6). It was when sons, daughters, young and old, experienced a personal relationship with Almighty God. It was a time when humans and animals interacted together without any fear. The spirit of the Lord interacted with the earth's inhabitants, through the saints, through visions, through dreams, and prophecy.

The Second Death

Rev. 2:11   He that hath an ear, let him hear what the Spirit saith unto the churches; He that overcometh shall not be hurt of the second death.

Rev. 20:6   Blessed and holy *is* he that hath part in the first resurrection: on such the second death hath no power, but they shall be priests of God and of Christ, and shall reign with him a thousand years

Rev. 20:14   And death and hell were cast into the lake of fire. This is the second death.

Rev. 21:8   But the fearful, and unbelieving, and the abominable, and murderers, and whoremongers, and sorcerers, and idolaters, and all liars, shall have their part in the lake which burneth with fire and brimstone: which is the second death.

Scripture mentions the *Second Death* four times is the KJV of the Bible. What is the Second Death? It is the Second Resurrection. The First Resurrection occurs between the end of the Tribulation Period and the beginning of the Millennium. The saints that have a part in the First Resurrection will not be affected by the Second Death or Second Resurrection. The implication is the Second Resurrection or Second Death occurs sometime after the Millennium. The Second Death is when the Millennial saints receive their rewards, and all corrupt individuals receive permanent confinement in the Lake of Fire that's fueled by brimstone.

The Second Death will not affect the saints. It is reserved for all ungodly beings, beginning with Satan from the spiritual realm and human beings from the earthly realm. The list is long and distinguished. It includes Satan, fallen angels, kings, presidents, priests, prophets, evangelists, pastors, unsavory individuals, etc. Before the Second Death, the Antichrist and the False Prophet are the first to experience the Lake of Fire. They'll take up residency there immediately after the Battle of Armageddon.

The timing of the Second Death is sometime after the Millennium is complete. Remember, Satan's imprisonment of one thousand years. After his release, he will roam the earth for a *Little Season*. Once he assembles a mighty army, he will mount a campaign against God, where he is defeated. Then, at the Great White Throne Judgment, the Lord sentences Satan and all of his ungodly followers to spend eternity in the Lake of Fire.

The Great White Throne Judgment

Rev. 20:11   And I saw a great white throne, and him that sat on it, from whose face the earth and the heaven fled away; and there was found no place for them.

Rev. 20:12   And I saw the dead, small and great, stand before God; and the books were opened: and another book was opened, which is *the book* of life: and the dead were judged out of those things which were written in the books, according to their works.

Rev. 20:13   And the sea gave up the dead which were in it; and death and hell delivered up the dead which were in them: and they were judged every man according to their works.

Rev. 20:14   And death and hell were cast into the lake of fire. This is the second death.

Rev. 20:15   And whosoever was not found written in the book of life was cast into the lake of fire.

The Great White Throne Judgment is the second and final resurrection. It is also known as the Second Death. It is a culmination of life, death, and the final judgment of all righteous and ungodly beings, both earthly and heavenly. The Great White Throne Judgment is when all the bodies of the faithful individuals from the Millennium are resurrected and transformed into glorified bodies. They join the ranks of the saints that took part in the First Resurrection.

On the contrary, Satan and all corrupt individuals that ever lived on the face of the earth receive permanent confinement in the Lake of Fire. It is a maximum-security facility where all ungodly beings receive torment day and night forever. The Great White Throne Judgment is definitive. It channels every individual's soul to its eternal destination.

God will sit on His throne in judgment. All the individuals that previously experienced physical death, but did not have a part in the First Resurrection, will stand before him. The Book of Life opens, and everyone who has his name recorded in it will receive new bodies. The Lord opens the other books and dispenses rewards or penalties to every individual based on those books' contents.

Notice the differences between the Book of Life and the other books. The Book of Life records the names of the saints. The other books record the deeds of man. Romans 2:6 states, "Who will render to every man according to his deeds." The Book of Life, which is singular, contrasts with the other books, which is plural. Because there is one Book of Life and several other books; this parallels with the words of Jesus. Matthew 7:13-14 states, "For wide *is* the gate, and broad *is* the way, that leadeth to destruction, and many there be which go in thereat ... strait *is* the gate, and narrow *is* the way, which leadeth unto life, and few there be that find it."

Mal. 3:16   Then they that feared the LORD spake often one to another: and the LORD hearkened, and heard *it*, and a book of remembrance was written before him for them that feared the LORD, and that thought upon his name.

Mal. 3:17   And they shall be mine, saith the LORD of hosts, in that day when I make up my jewels; and I will spare them, as a man spareth his own son that serveth him.

Mal. 3:18   Then shall ye return, and discern between the righteous and the wicked, between him that serveth God and him that serveth him not.

Scripture references another book known as the Book of Remembrance. This book is comparable to the Book of Life. This book records the names of individuals that fear the Lord and continually meditate on His name. The inscription of their names in the Book of Remembrance signifies that God will remember their faithfulness. The Lord will look after them as jewels. He will look upon them as He looks upon His Son. Just as His Son will rule and reign, He will also grant them the right to discern between the righteous deeds and the wicked deeds of the ones-left-behind.

Psa. 69:28   Let them be blotted out of the book of the living, and not be written with the righteous.

The Lord will not record the names of unrighteous individuals (spiritually dead) in the same book as the righteous individuals (spiritually alive). There are several books associated with godly individuals, and they are the Book of Life, the Book of Remembrance, and the Book of the Living. Although the books have different names, their respective titles describe the destiny of those individuals whose names the books contain. The Book of Life records those that will experience life after death. The Book of Remembrance records those that Jesus will remember when He establishes His everlasting kingdom. The Book of the Living records those that will live with Christ in His eternal kingdom. It appears that there are three separate and distinct books, but in all actuality, they are all the same book. The Book of Life is the Book of Remembrance and the Book of the Living. The other books referenced in Revelation 20:12 contains all of the deeds of humanity in its entirety.

Recording Names in the Book of Life

Act. 3:19   Repent ye therefore, and be converted, that your sins may be blotted out, when the times of refreshing shall come from the presence of the Lord;

Rom. 10:9   That if thou shalt confess with thy mouth the Lord Jesus, and shalt believe in thine heart that God hath raised him from the dead, thou shalt be saved.

Rom. 10:10 For with the heart man believeth unto righteousness; and with the mouth confession is made unto salvation.

There is only one way for individuals to have their name recorded in the Book of Life. He or she must believe and repent. First, one must believe that Jesus Christ is the one and only Savior of man. Second, he must repent or convert his or her way of thinking from unrighteousness to righteousness. Repentance is synonymous with being born-again. Repentance is a lifestyle change, which becomes an outward act of confession. Repentance is the only way for an individual to get his name inscribed in the Book of Life.

Exo. 32:33 And the LORD said unto Moses, Whosoever hath sinned against me, him will I blot out of my book.

Psa. 69:28 Let them be blotted out of the book of the living, and not be written with the righteous.

Contrary to popular belief, just because the Lamb's Book of Life has a name recorded in it, that does not guarantee that it will remain there forever. Scripture points out that just as a man gets his name recorded, The Lord can erase it as well. The following are some scriptures that support the blotting out of names from the Book of Life.

Exo. 32:33 And the LORD said unto Moses, Whosoever hath sinned against me, him will I blot out of my book.

Deu. 29:20 The LORD will not spare him, but then the anger of the LORD and his jealousy shall smoke against that man, and all the curses that are written in this book shall lie upon him, and the LORD shall blot out his name from under heaven.

Rev. 3:5   He that overcometh, the same shall be clothed in white raiment; and I will not blot out his name out of the book of life, but I will confess his name before my Father, and before his angels.

Protocol forbids recording of the names of unrighteous individuals in the same book that contains the names of the righteous individuals. For that reason, if the Lord records an individual's name in the Book of Life and for some reason, he becomes reprobate and commits the Unpardonable Sin, the Lord can blot out his name from the Book of Life. The Lord bases an individual's final judgment upon his deeds that the *other books* contain.

There are several different viewpoints about the timing of the literal recording of an individual's names in the Book of Life. Some think the name of a person is recorded in the Book of Life when he is born. Others believe documenting an individual's name in the Book of Life takes place when he's born-again. Scriptures don't say verbatim when the Lord records the name in the Book of Life, but it declares that an individual must be born-again to experience eternal life. John 3:3 states, "Except a man be born again, he cannot see the kingdom of God." Stating that one must be born-again indicates that he has already attained physical birth but has not yet acquired spiritual birth. If it's true that one must be born-again, then that lends to the idea that the Lord does not record one's name in the Book of Life at birth, but He records it in the Book of Life at repentance.

Isa. 62:3   Thou shalt also be a crown of glory in the hand of the LORD, and a royal diadem in the hand of thy God.

1Co. 2:9   But as it is written, Eye hath not seen, nor ear heard, neither have entered into the heart of man, the things which God hath prepared for them that love him.

Even though every individual who has his name written in the Book of Life is now experiencing a beautiful relationship with the Lord, it is nothing compared to the face-to-face interconnection that awaits them in the Lord's eternal kingdom. Presently, the saints cannot comprehend the magnitude of the love of God that He has prepared for them. 1 Corinthians 2:9 states, "Eye hath not seen, nor ear heard, neither have entered into the heart of man, the things which God hath prepared for them that love him."

The saints will become kings and priests. Not only will they be crowned kings and priests, but they will also receive a crown of royalty, a crown of glory, and a crown of honor. They will become heirs with Christ. 1 Peter 5:4 states, "When the chief Shepherd shall appear, ye shall receive a crown of glory that fadeth not away.

APPENDICES

APPENDIX A

PRETERISTS

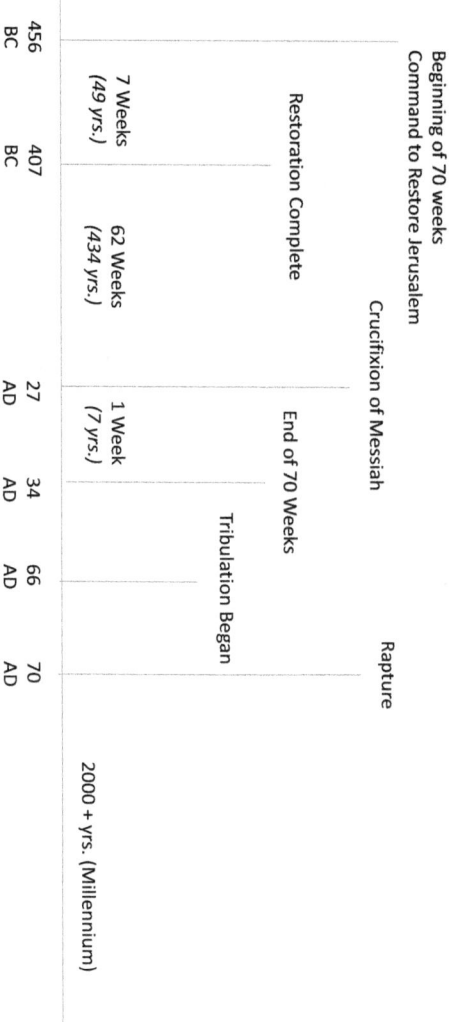

Timeline chart (rotated):

- 456 BC — Beginning of 70 weeks / Command to Restore Jerusalem
- 7 Weeks (49 yrs.)
- 407 BC — Restoration Complete
- 62 Weeks (434 yrs.)
- 27 AD — Crucifixion of Messiah
- 1 Week (7 yrs.)
- 34 AD — End of 70 Weeks
- 66 AD — Tribulation Began
- 70 AD — Rapture
- 2000 + yrs. (Millennium)

APPENDIX B

FUTURISTS

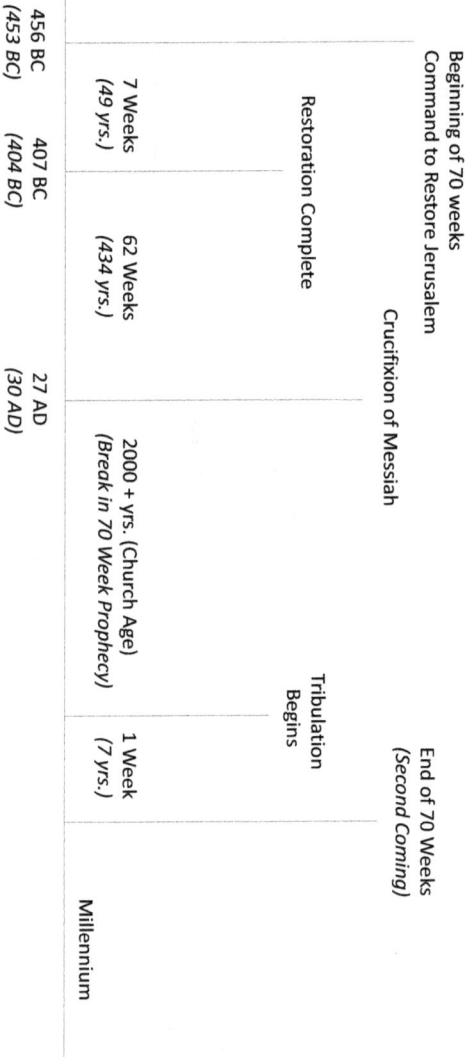

APPENDIX C

PARTIAL PRETERIST

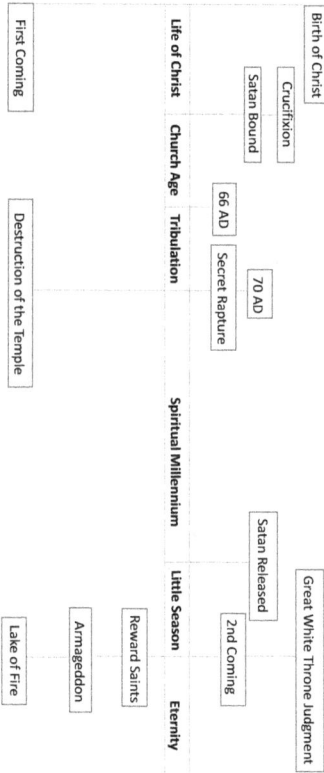

First Coming

Life of Christ

Birth of Christ

Crucifixion

Satan Bound

Church Age

66 AD

Tribulation

70 AD

Secret Rapture

Destruction of the Temple

Spiritual Millennium

Satan Released

Little Season

2nd Coming

Great White Throne Judgment

Reward Saints

Eternity

Armageddon

Lake of Fire

APPENDIX D

FULL PRETERIST

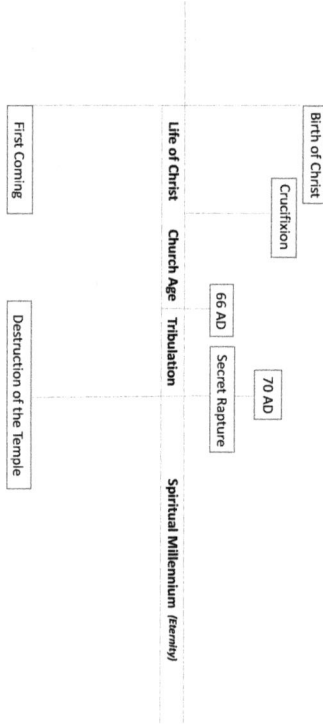

Birth of Christ

Crucifixion

Life of Christ

First Coming

Church Age

66 AD

70 AD

Tribulation

Secret Rapture

Destruction of the Temple

Spiritual Millennium *(Eternity)*

APPENDIX E

PRE-WRATH

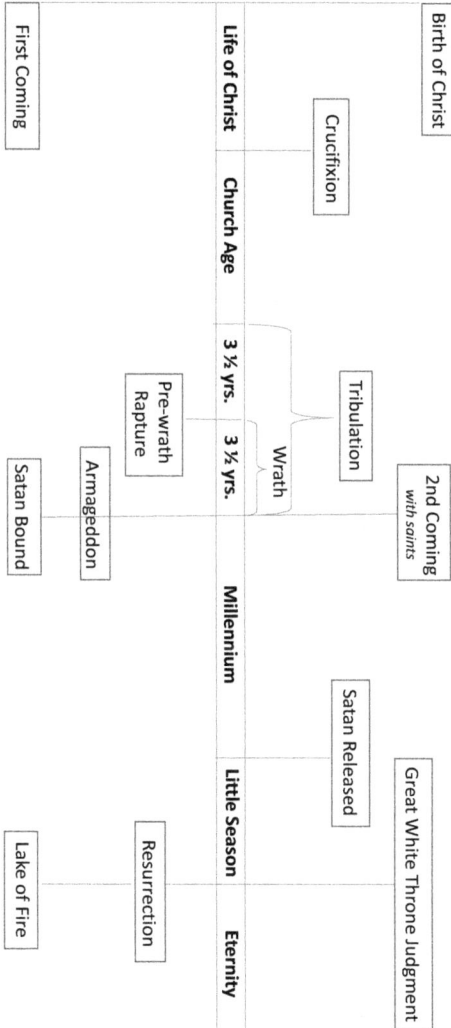

APPENDIX F

PRE-TRIBULATION

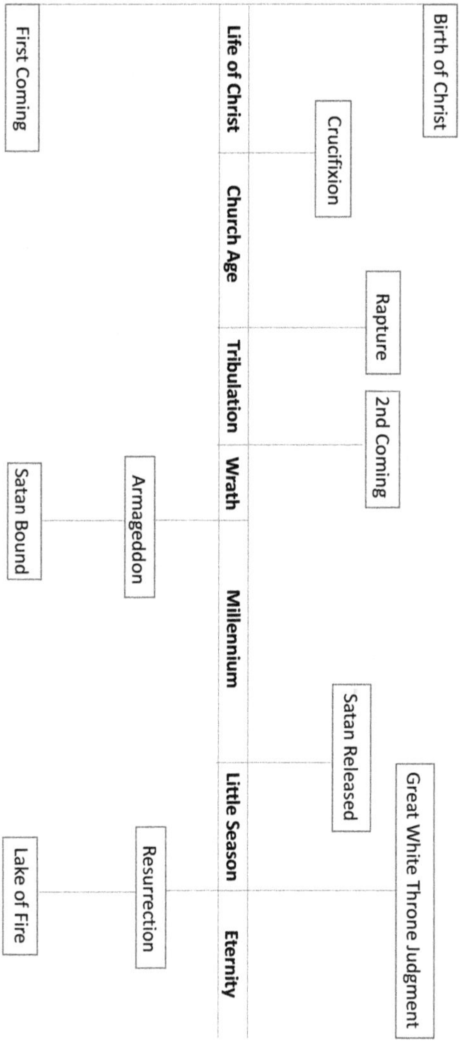

Birth of Christ
First Coming
Life of Christ
Crucifixion
Church Age
Rapture
Tribulation
2nd Coming
Wrath
Armageddon
Satan Bound
Millennium
Satan Released
Little Season
Great White Throne Judgment
Resurrection
Lake of Fire
Eternity

APPENDIX G

MID-TRIBULATION

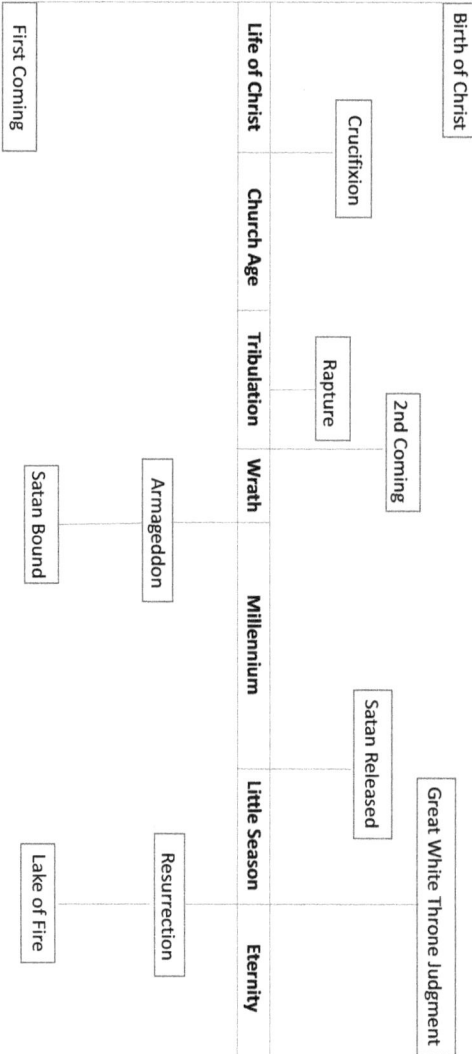

Birth of Christ

First Coming

Life of Christ

Crucifixion

Church Age

Tribulation

Rapture

2nd Coming

Wrath

Satan Bound

Armageddon

Millennium

Satan Released

Great White Throne Judgment

Little Season

Resurrection

Lake of Fire

Eternity

APPENDIX H

POST-TRIBULATION

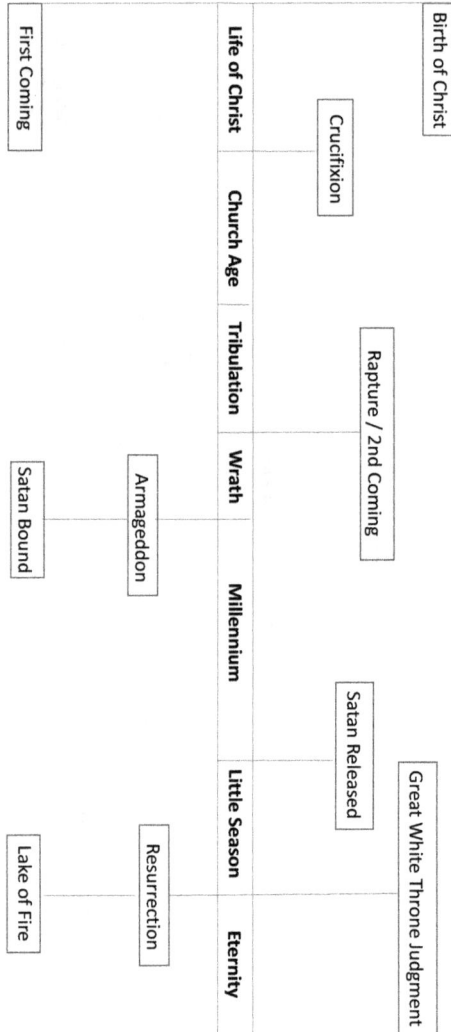

Birth of Christ

Life of Christ

Crucifixion

First Coming

Church Age

Tribulation

Rapture / 2nd Coming

Wrath

Armageddon

Satan Bound

Millennium

Satan Released

Little Season

Great White Throne Judgment

Resurrection

Lake of Fire

Eternity

APPENDIX I

A-MILLENNIUM

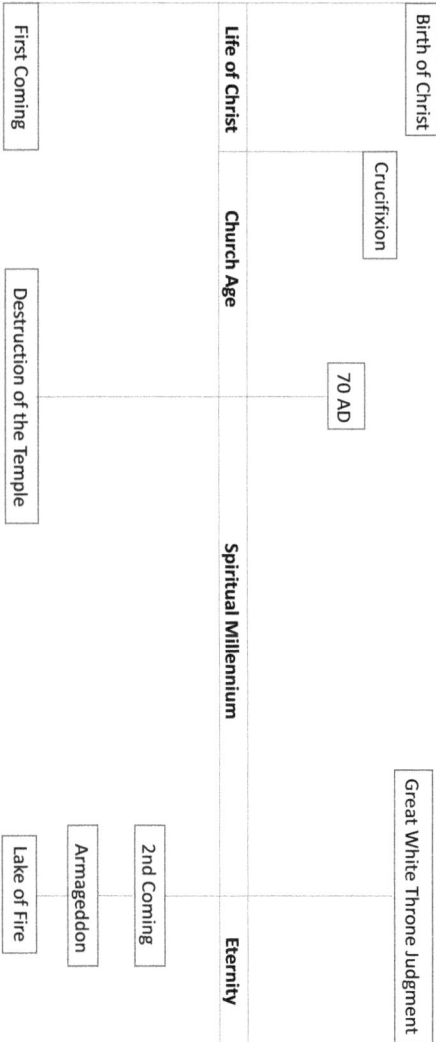

APPENDIX J

PRE-MILLENNIUM

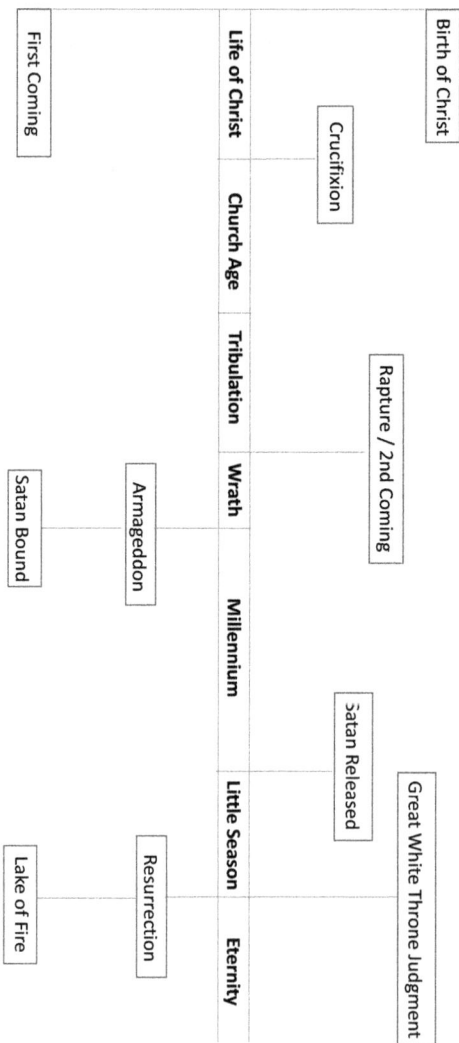

Birth of Christ								
	Life of Christ	Church Age	Tribulation	Wrath	Millennium	Little Season	Eternity	

- First Coming
- Crucifixion
- Rapture / 2nd Coming
- Satan Bound
- Armageddon
- Satan Released
- Great White Throne Judgment
- Lake of Fire
- Resurrection

APPENDIX K

POST-MILLENNIUM

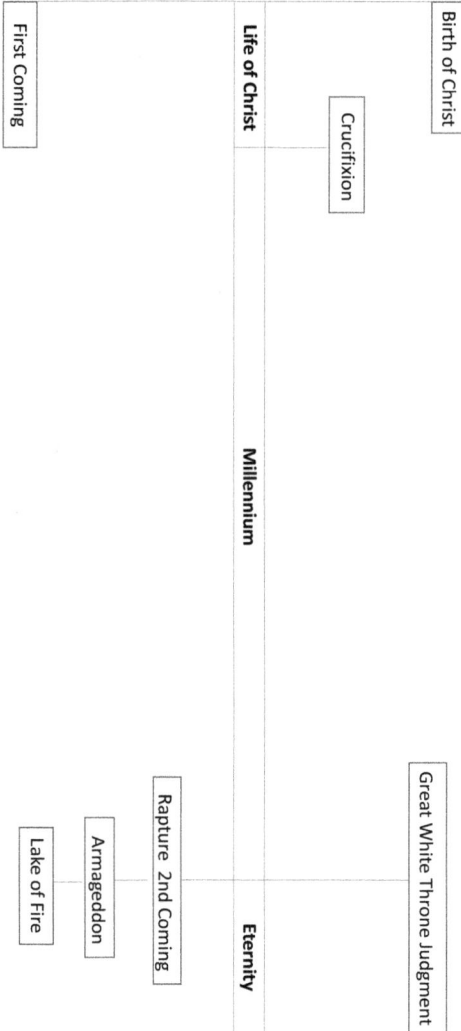

Birth of Christ

Life of Christ

Crucifixion

First Coming

Millennium

Great White Throne Judgment

Rapture 2nd Coming

Armageddon

Lake of Fire

Eternity

ABOUT THE AUTHOR

CHARLES THOMPSON has been living the life of a visionary for years. As he sees a need, he establishes a vision for how things should be, and then has put a track record in place for how to achieve the desired results. In the early 1980s, Charles recognized that New York City wasn't the place where he wanted to raise his three young daughters, so he made preparations get a transfer to Tampa, Florida. It didn't matter that they didn't know a soul in Florida or that they had never been there. He, his wife, and his three young daughters picked up, moved, and made a home there. He and the family have been living in the greater Tampa Bay area ever since.

A few years after living in Tampa, Charles recognized that the neighborhood his family was living in was changing for the worse, and he wanted better for his family. So he bought a piece of land in a sparsely populated neighborhood north of Tampa, and proceeded to build a house for his family. It didn't matter that he was a mailman by trade, and didn't have any contracting experience. He built his family a house, and 30 years later, he still lives in that house with his wife Sandra.

So when in 2007, after 25 years of walking with Christ and studying the Word, it should have come as no surprise that Charles would have established another vision as a solution for a problem. During his years of walking with Christ, Charles noticed that many believers didn't actually comprehend the Bible's message. Sure, they went to traditional churches, and heard the sermons, but for a variety of reasons, they knew very little about the Word. As such, they often had trouble putting its principles into action in their daily lives. Because of these nuances, and being inspired by the Holy Spirit, Epistle of Christ Ministries was established with the goal of teaching the Word of God to those who are looking for greater spiritual growth and understanding.

www.ingramcontent.com/pod-product-compliance
Lightning Source LLC
Chambersburg PA
CBHW051959090426
42741CB00008B/1471